Words of Praise for *The Pep Talk*

"There is no doubt in my mind one of the reasons we turned the program around at The University of Miami was Kevin Elko. His 'Pep Talks' taught players valuable lessons about focusing, handling adversity as well as success. Kevin had a major impact on the entire program. This book will show you how winning is done."

—Butch Davis, Former Head Football Coach, University of Miami and Cleveland Browns, Head Coach, University of North Carolina

"In *The Pep Talk* Elko and Shook reveal that winning comes from within. This is true on and off the football field. This is one of the most inspirational books I have ever read. I highly recommend it as 'must reading.'"

—Larry Coker, Former Head Football Coach, University of Miami

"Dr. Kevin Elko is one of the brightest men I know. He will help you focus your organization, your team, and your life."

—Steve Pederson, Athletic Director, University of Nebraska

"Dr. Kevin Elko is one of the most inspirational and positive people I have ever been privileged to know. No matter how often I watch Dr. Elko work he inspires me. Kevin has done it to me again in *The Pep Talk*, providing a life lesson and a great message applicable to all walks of life. This book is a must read."

—Tom Donahoe, President and General Manager, Buffalo Bills

You can read this story in an afternoon and like the boys on the team in Lincoln, Ohio, its impact will stay with you for years to come.

—John David Mann, coauthor of *You Call The Shots* and *The Go-Giver*

Although I had never played football, *The Pep Talk* spoke directly to me . . . it addresses the best in human nature, providing the inspiration we need to make our lives and those with whom we work much better. I recommend the book very highly.

—Dr. Gordon Gee, president, Ohio State University

"I loved this book. It has a great message for every man, woman, and child."
—Bill Callahan, Former Head Football Coach,
University of Nebraska and Oakland Raiders

THE
PEP TALK

THE
PEP TALK

A Football Story about
THE BUSINESS OF WINNING

DR. KEVIN ELKO
and ROBERT L. SHOOK

THOMAS NELSON
Since 1798

NASHVILLE DALLAS MEXICO CITY RIO DE JANEIRO BEIJING

Published in Nashville, Tennessee, by Thomas Nelson. Thomas Nelson is a registered trademark of Thomas Nelson, Inc.

Thomas Nelson, Inc., titles may be purchased in bulk for educational, business, fund-raising, or sales promotional use. For information, please e-mail SpecialMarkets@ThomasNelson.com.

Unless otherwise noted, Scripture quotations are taken from the NEW REVISED STANDARD VERSION of the Bible. © 1989 by the Division of Christian Education of the National Council of the Churches of Christ in the U.S.A. All rights reserved.

Library of Congress Cataloging-in-Publication Data

Elko, Kevin, 1958–
    The pep talk / Kevin Elko and Robert L. Shook.
      p. cm.
    ISBN 978-1-59555-121-4
    ISBN 978-1-59555-194-8 (IE)
    1. Life skills. 2. Self-help techniques. I. Shook, Robert L., 1938- II. Title.
HQ2075.E55 2008
658.4'092—dc22

2007037263

Printed in the United States of America
08 09 10 11 QWM 1 2 3 4 5 6

To Karen, whose love, everyday, is my Pep Talk.
—KEVIN

To Michael, Sarah, Sawyer and Avery
—WITH MUCH LOVE, RLS

CONTENTS

INTRODUCTION

At some point in your life, you've probably sat through a pep talk. Certainly if you played high school or college sports, you've been subjected to your share. You may have even heard one when you attended a sales meeting or a business conference. If so, when you sit in on the one given to the Lincoln Lions in the following pages, you'll realize that this is not your garden-variety pep talk—it's an Elko pep talk.

The Lincoln Lions are a fictitious high school football team with a twenty-four-game losing streak. The story begins the day before their final game of the 1975 season against the Jacktown Giants, the formidable, undefeated state champions in Ohio. Although the plot and characters are fictional, "The Pep Talk" itself is based on exactly what Kevin Elko says when he addresses NFL teams and Division One football teams. But our story goes beyond the pep talk, and we see the lasting effects that it has on three players.

Kevin earns an annual seven-figure income for giving pep talks to NFL teams such as the Pittsburgh Steelers, Miami Dolphins, New Orleans Saints, Cleveland Browns, Buffalo Bills, Dallas Cowboys, and Philadelphia Eagles. He has also worked with such powerhouse college teams as the Miami Hurricanes, Nebraska Cornhuskers, Pittsburgh Panthers, Georgia Tech Yellow Jackets, and the Louisiana State University Tigers. He has an impressive résumé and a reputation as the best in his profession. As a testament to his effectiveness, Kevin is the proud owner of three NFL championship rings.

Be assured that the pep talk you are about to read is indeed the real thing. The setting and characters may be fictitious, but the words in this book are what you'd hear if you were listening to Kevin in an NFL locker room. However, you don't have to be a football player to reap the benefits of a great pep talk.

Robert L. Shook

The town of Lincoln, Ohio, was no longer the boom-town it had been in the early 1950s, back when steel was king. Peaking at 23,500 in 1954 (the year before the River Steel Corporation shut down), Lincoln's population had fallen below the 18,000 mark by the early '70s. Nothing ever replaced the high-paying jobs earned in the steel mill. Those who remained had to settle for lower-paying employment; you could say that they got "McDonalded."

There was also a time in the '50s when Lincoln High's beloved Lions were a football dynasty. For proof you can check out the glass showcase in the hall of the school's main entrance. There, proudly exhibited for posterity, are Lincoln's '50, '52, and '53 state championship trophies; these polished bronze relics serve as a reminder to the community's young people of its proud heritage. Each autumn, old-timers can be seen huddling at local joints and taverns, reminiscing about the good old days—when steel was king and the Lions reigned supreme.

Times have since been lean in Lincoln. The mill permanently closed its doors, and the mighty Lions' roar is but an echo—not one win in twenty-four straight outings. Friday night's game on November 7, 1975, was unlikely to be any different. It was the school's last game of the season, and coming to town were the Jacktown Giants, a formidable foe heavily favored to win their forty-second consecutive game. It seemed inevitable that Jacktown would win another state championship, making it a record four straight. Ranked the nation's third best high school football team by *Sports Illustrated*, Jacktown had outscored opponents by a margin of 37 points a game. Ohio sportscasters were touting this year's squad as the state's all-time greatest team. Their final regular season opponent, Lincoln, had scored only five touchdowns during its pitiful 0–7 season.

Having been hung in effigy after the previous week's humiliating 28–0 loss to longtime rival Middleburg (1–6), Coach Jack Morris fully understood that his coaching job was on the line. It mattered little that in his early coaching years he had twice taken the team to the state regionals. Nor, for that matter, did anyone give a hoot that he had been the school's two-time all-state running back in the early 1950s. He'd had such promise then . . .

Jack Morris had been a second-team All–Big Ten halfback during his junior year at Ohio State. As a senior, a knee injury

2

during a scrimmage abruptly ended his playing career just one week before the start of the season. While Morris stoically accepted his fate as "part of the game," the folks in Lincoln viewed his abrupt departure from the sport as nothing short of a tragedy. After all, Fred Jones, the *Lincoln Gazette*'s whiz sports reporter, had touted Lincoln's favorite son for All-American honors and an early pick in the NFL draft.

Now in his fourteenth season as head coach, Jack remembered the days when he was the most popular man in Lincoln—back when he first coached the team and was still recognized as a glorified gridiron god. Back then, Morris could have run for mayor and been a shoo-in. But he had opted for a bigger job. He knew that in small-town Ohio, the townsfolk's highest regard went to the winning head coach. Over the years, he had learned just how important the *winning* part of that title was.

It was 6:15 on Thursday morning, approximately thirty-six hours before the Lincoln-Jacktown game. Jack Morris sat alone in a booth at Abe's Lincoln Diner, reading the *Lincoln Gazette*. Now forty-three, Jack looked very much like a small-town high school football coach. He wore a blue and white nylon jacket that had a large golden lion emblazoned on the back with the words "Lincoln Lions" running through it. His matching cap flaunted the same emblem. On the front upper left side of his jacket, small gold letters identified him as "head coach," a title that should carry with it the status of "The Man." However, on this particular morning, Coach Morris had no strut to his walk. A twenty-four-game losing streak doesn't exactly generate confidence, particularly when you're coaching the worst team in your school's history, and tomorrow night you'll be facing arguably the best Ohio high school football team ever assembled.

The diner was a popular breakfast spot for local businessmen, frequented by lawyers, accountants, judges, and other Lincoln notables. At certain tables you would find the same occupants at the same time every day of the workweek, some even on Saturdays. Although there were no reserved tables, the regular customers knew who sat where: A group of insurance salesmen occupied the second booth from the front door. The fourth booth belonged to the bankers, the fifth to the chamber of commerce, and so on. Some of the customers had been eating at Abe's with the same group of friends for decades, joining in the "breakfast with the boys" ritual of thousands of small towns across America. Conversations ranged from local weather conditions and politics to high school football. Abe Horowitz, the owner of the establishment, was a self-proclaimed sports addict, with years of sports paraphernalia adorning the cedar-paneled walls.

"Up a little early this morning, huh, Coach?" Beatrice, a matronly waitress, asked.

"Wanted to beat the crowd," he answered. "Frankly, with tomorrow night's Jacktown game, I'm not in the mood to hear a bunch of old-timers tell me how to coach our boys."

"The way those men get on your case," Beatrice said, "I'm surprised you even come in here every morning."

"It's the coffee, Beatrice. Besides, I usually don't let them get to me. But this morning, I figured it wouldn't hurt to get here half an hour before they do."

An energetic man dressed in a dark suit walked into the diner. In his late thirties, he was a stranger to Lincoln. Few young men wore suits in this workingman's town (the older men who did acquired the habit in the '50s), and Jack Morris knew those who did. But it was not only the suit that tagged this man a stranger in town. He also wore a late 1960s tweed snap-brim grey and black fedora, complete with a red feather in the hatband. Such a hat was bound to get attention. In Lincoln, baseball caps were the norm.

The man could have sat anywhere. At the counter, a booth, or a table. Jack Morris was the only customer in the place. But instead, the stranger walked directly to the booth where Morris sipped on his hot coffee.

"Good morning, Coach Morris, the name is Christopher," the man beamed, extending his hand and following through with a hearty handshake. "I'm a traveling man passing through your fine burg. I happen to be a big high school football fan, and I know, come Friday night, you are up against a tough adversary. I'd like to help your team in tomorrow's game against Jacktown. Mind if I join you for a cup of coffee?"

"It's a free country, and I'm not going anywhere until I finish my coffee," Morris sighed, "so pull up a seat, and take a load off the ground."

The stranger sat down. He didn't bother to take off his hat.

Of course, Morris didn't notice it at the time, and why should he? He always wore his cap in the diner.

After the two men exchanged pleasantries, Morris asked, "You're not from around here, are you, Mr. Christopher? If I were to guess, I'd have to say you come from the East."

"Yes, sir," the stranger answered. "Born and raised in Bethlehem, Pennsylvania. Live outside Philadelphia today."

"The City of Brotherly Love," Morris said.

"Right again, my friend. But Bethlehem, now there's an interesting place. It's a steel town much like Lincoln once was. At one time Bethlehem made claim to the world's largest steel works. However, and much more interesting in some circles, we're better known for producing great athletes. Bethlehem is in Lehigh Valley, a real hotbed for breeding big-time sports stars. Hundreds of them over the years. NFL Football Hall of Fame member Chuck Bednarik is a favorite son. And so are baseball's pitching legend Curt Simmons; racecar driver Mario Andretti; and heavyweight boxer Larry Holmes. Each and every one of those fine athletes hails from the Lehigh Valley."

"I'm familiar with the area's reputation," Morris acknowledged. "I read about it now and then in my sports magazines."

"You were quite a star in your youth," Mr. Christopher added. "I saw you play against Michigan in the Big Shoe. I felt like crying when I first learned about your knee injury. Now about the game tomorrow . . ."

"You did say something about giving us help, didn't you?"

Morris interrupted. "You really think you can help us? We've been playing some pretty pitiful football."

"You heard me right."

"What exactly do you have in mind, Mr. Christopher?"

"A pep talk."

"A pep talk?"

"That's right. I'd like to give a twenty-five-minute pep talk to the team following this afternoon's practice," Mr. Christopher said. "I've given my share of pep talks to many high school and college football players, Coach. I might add that I once gave a talk to the Philadelphia Eagles and another time to the Cleveland Browns. The teams I've addressed have done quite well. Although I can't guarantee a winner every time, at the very least, I can promise you that I'll give your boys a good solid message that will work for them on and off the field. Yes, sir, it will be something that will serve them well over the years ahead."

Trying to size up the stranger, Morris stared at Mr. Christopher in wonderment. Was this man for real or some kind of a nut case?

"Don't you agree, my friend," Mr. Christopher continued, "that's what coaching young people is truly all about? Giving them something that will stay with them after their football days are long gone."

"You won't get an argument from me, Mr. Christopher. However, the long term is sometimes overlooked in football towns in this neck of the woods. Winning is all that matters to the good citizens of Lincoln. They take football very seriously and very personally in this town. It's a matter of pride. In a way, it's how the community has come to define itself. Traditionally, a winning football team was part of who we were in Lincoln. The winning attitude went well beyond the football field. It's deeply engrained in the community's culture. People around here used to believe that if you lived in Lincoln, good fortune came your way because we were people who knew how to win. Now, with the steel mill shut down, jobs have become as scarce as hen's teeth and those to be had don't pay much.

"'At least we got our great football tradition,' people would say," Morris added. "But now, it's become a losing football tradition. Lincoln is no longer about winning. I'm afraid we look at ourselves as losers—the combination of the poor economy and a poor performance on the football field has dealt this town a double whammy."

"Yes, my friend, I know all about Lincoln's glory days," Mr. Christopher said. "Just outside the valley there'd be clouds of smoke in the horizon above Lincoln, and it was a sign that times were good. It was telling you: 'Welcome to Lincoln. Everyone is working and business is booming.' But once the sky turned crystal clean, it's as if it were saying, 'Stay away. Business stinks and everyone here is in a bad mood.'"

Glancing at his watch, Morris said, "Let's get back to the main subject. Now, you said you had a pep talk that would help us whip Jacktown?"

"Coach, I never promise a win," Mr. Christopher said. "I

just don't do that. But I can promise you that I will make a positive difference in the lives of your players. I suggest we just concentrate on the players, and let's not worry about the townsfolk. Let's focus on what we can do for those fine young boys on your squad. I know I can tell them some wonderful things that will work in their favor. Guidance that goes far beyond the football field. And who knows, we might just win. Didn't David slay Goliath?"

"You know, Mr. Christopher, I don't know why, but something inside me tells me you might do my boys some good."

"I promise you that I will, and I am a man of my word, Coach. What time do you want me today?"

"Let's say 5:30," Morris answered, a little reluctantly. "Yeah, be at the locker room at 5:30, Mr. Christopher."

The afternoon practice was uneventful. The players went through the motions without much enthusiasm. Although it remained unspoken, everyone knew that it was only a matter of how much the Giants would run up the score. There was no thought about winning the game; instead, everyone was thinking about how the team could "stay in the game" and save face. It seemed they agreed with Bill Franklin, a local *Lincoln Gazette* sportswriter who wrote, "A close game, say, losing by a margin of three touchdowns or less, will be considered a moral victory for the Lions."

"My old man says that when he played for Lincoln, they always whipped Jacktown," one player muttered in the locker room.

"Yeah, and ever since it has been payback time for Jacktown, because every time we're up against them they kick our butts from here to next Sunday."

An oversized lineman raised the conversation to another level. "Who here is dreading tomorrow's game as much as I am?" he shouted from a standing position on the bench, shaking his entire body to portray "the willies" they were all feeling.

"Knock it off, you guys. Here comes the coach."

Coach Morris walked in with the stranger and stood in the locker room facing the players. "Good practice, guys. Now, before you head home I want you to gather over here because I've got a special guest today who's going to say a few words to you about tomorrow's game. This is Mr. Christopher, a man who has spoken to high school and college teams all over the Midwest. He was even brought in once to speak to the Cleveland Browns. Now while he speaks, I don't want anyone opening his big mouth." He said as he eyed the red-faced linebacker. "I want you to show our guest the same respect that I expect you to show me."

THE PEP TALK

Still dressed in a suit, Mr. Christopher stood facing the players. He never took off his suit jacket nor did he remove his fedora. With his left hand, he held up a football in the air until there was complete silence. Then he spoke.

"There were two buffaloes that were standing in the open range in Wyoming when a couple of cowboys on horseback trotted by. One cowboy said to the other, 'Look at those two buffaloes. They've got to be the ugliest animals on the entire range.'

"'Yeah, look at their big heads on their skinny bodies,' the other cowboy said. 'And you know, I'm told buffaloes are as stupid as they are ugly.'

"That's when one buffalo said to the other buffalo, 'I thought that out here, home on the range, we're not supposed to hear a discouraging word.'"

A couple of players snickered, but most of them didn't crack a smile. The joke simply went over their heads.

"Gentlemen, I overheard some of you talking to each other in the locker room, and I couldn't help hearing some of you saying some discouraging words about tomorrow night's game. Sure, you are playing one terrific football team, but remember that they're high school kids—just like you guys. They're not the Ohio State Buckeyes. They're not the Cleveland Browns."

It was as if Mr. Christopher made eye contact with every player in the room. And as if in unison, all eyes looked down.

"The Bible tells us in Numbers chapter thirteen," the speaker said, "that Moses sent twelve men to the land of Canaan, commanding them to spy on the enemy. 'Go up there into the hill country,' Moses instructed them, 'and see what the land is like, and whether the people who live in it are strong or weak, whether they are few or many.'

"Upon their return, the spies reported back to Moses, 'All the people we saw in it are of great size.' They claimed that the Canaanites were so large that in comparison they felt as small as grasshoppers. The Canaanites, however, were not giants. To lead his people into the land of milk and honey, Moses recognized that he must inspire them to see themselves worthy of possessing it.

"I don't see any grasshoppers in this room. If you think of yourself as a grasshopper, please raise your hand. How about you, Jimmy, are you a grasshopper? Or you over in the back. Are you, Henry?"

"No sir," Jimmy answered, seeming surprised that the stranger knew his name. Henry just shook his head.

"Okay, so there are no grasshoppers in this room. I'm glad we got that out of the way.

"The Giants are not giants. Remember, men, in order to win at anything, the winning starts up here in your head. If you think otherwise, you defeat yourself before the game starts. I don't think you want to spot Jacktown three touchdowns before you step onto the field. Well, that's exactly what happens when you convince yourself that you can't win.

IN ORDER TO WIN AT ANYTHING, THE WINNING MUST START IN YOUR HEAD.

"In Joshua 1:9, the Bible tells us: 'Be strong and courageous; do not be frightened or dismayed, for the LORD your God is with you wherever you go.'"

"I repeat: Be strong. Be courageous. Don't be afraid. God is with you."

It was the second time that the stranger quoted from the Bible. It seemed to get everyone's attention. But it was out of context. Evidently, they never heard a biblical quotation in a locker room.

"There's a story about a Stanford math student who was doing graduate work during the Depression," the stranger said. "His professor announced to the class, 'Whoever scores the highest grade on this Wednesday's final examination will be offered the job as my teaching assistant.'

"The student was financially strapped and desperately needed the job to stay in school. He studied so hard that he overslept on the day of the exam and walked into class ten minutes late. The professor handed him the exam that consisted of eight math problems. Two problems were also handwritten on the blackboard. The student did his best to complete the exam, but time ran out before he got around to answering the two problems on the board.

"'I didn't have time to do those two questions,' he said to the professor, pointing to the blackboard, 'and I really need that job.'

"'You've got until Friday to turn in your answers for those two questions,' the professor answered, but come Friday, that's it.'

"The appreciative student profusely thanked the professor, copied what was written on the blackboard, and headed home. He worked on them day and night. By Friday morning, he woke up with just a couple of hours of sleep, finished the test, and rushed to his professor's office with his completed assignment.

"The next morning at 7:00, the student heard a loud knock on his door. When he went to the door, there stood his math professor.

"Upon letting him in, the professor said, 'Congratulations, you just made mathematics history.'

"'What do you mean?'

"'Those two problems on the board,' the professor said. 'I wrote them on the board before you arrived and told the class that nobody has ever been able to solve them. Not even Albert

Einstein. Had you been there on time, you would have known they weren't part of the test.'

"The student acknowledged that had he known the truth, he would have never attempted to answer them."

Mr. Christopher paused for a few moments to let the thought sink in. This time his audience got the message. Heads were nodding, and faint smiles appeared on the boys' faces. Then he continued.

"What if you didn't know that Jacktown had a record-breaking winning streak? What if you didn't know about your team's losing streak? What if you all believed that together, there was no limit to what you can do as a team?

"Nobody in this room should be thinking about the past. As Carl Sandburg said, 'The past is a bucket of ashes.' Forget about Jacktown's winning streak. Forget about Lincoln's losing streak. Throw those thoughts out of your mind. Why? Because they don't matter. The only thing that matters when you step onto the playing field tomorrow night is the game itself. You got that straight, Frankie?"

Mr. Christopher tossed the football to Frank Howard, a lineman and the biggest boy on the team. He caught the ball, immediately stood to attention, and said, "Yes, sir." Mr. Christopher motioned to him to throw back the football. Howard did and sat down.

"During a recent trip to Disneyland, I walked by a play that was in progress," Mr. Christopher told the players. "The park employees asked twenty volunteers from the audience to partic-ipate in the play; a mother and her five-year-old girl were among those who were brought up onto the stage. The little girl didn't have a hair on her head, and she was having the time of her life. Her mother was enjoying herself as much as her small daughter. I learned that they were special guests of Disney—the little girl had lost her hair because she had cancer and was being treated by chemotherapy. The little girl was dying, *so why were she and her mother so happy?* you may ask. They were so happy because they were in Disneyland, that's why.

"They made a choice. They could feel sorry for themselves, or they could enjoy their day at Disneyland. They chose to enjoy the day. They said, 'This is my day.' It was their responsibility. (By the way, if you break down the word *responsibility*, it means 'respond with ability.') Each of us has to decide how we are going to respond. You can decide how you want to respond tomorrow night. I suggest you do as that brave little girl and her loving mother did: They decided that they would seize the moment. They chose to say, 'This is my day, and I will make the most of it.' In tomorrow's game you can choose to say, 'This is my day and I will make the most of it.'"

THIS IS MY DAY AND I WILL MAKE THE MOST OF IT

Mr. Christopher had lowered his voice when he said, "This is my day, and I will make the most of it," and looked around the room. He saw that a few of the boys were teary-eyed: his message was reaching them.

"Jesus taught us in John 20:29: 'Blessed are those who have not seen and yet have come to believe.'

"Those were not idle words. It's easy to believe that you will win a game when you're riding a winning streak. Tonight, I am asking you to believe in yourselves and that you can beat Jacktown even though your past performances do not compare to theirs. This makes it harder to believe, doesn't it? I won't kid you. It's not going to be easy tomorrow night. It will be difficult. But you can do it. And you can start doing it by believing in yourself and in your teammates. This is something you can start to do right now. I want you all to stand up and tell the man next to you that you believe in him. And I want you to tell him *why* you believe in him. Go ahead, do it."

Everybody stood up and turned to someone next to him and they started talking to each other. Mr. Christopher let them talk for two minutes and then he instructed them to sit back down.

"There's a story about a fourteen-year-old boy who was born without a left arm. The boy told his mother that he wanted to take judo lessons. Reluctantly she enrolled him in a course. The instructor worked with the boy, and in particular, taught him one move. 'Master this move,' the boy was told again and again.

"The boy did as he was instructed and soon was winning matches; he qualified to compete in the final round of a major judo tournament. His opponent was a real brute who had overwhelmingly defeated his foes. Before the match, the referee pulled the instructor aside and said, 'You're going to get your boy killed. Even if he had two arms, he's no competition for this guy. He's a killer.'

"'Don't worry,' the instructor said. 'He'll be fine.'

"The boy even told his instructor, 'I'm going to get killed.'

"The instructor replied, 'You just do as I taught you, and there isn't anything to worry about.'

"The boy won the match. On the way home from the tournament, the boy said to his instructor, 'Why did you let me go into the ring with such a strong opponent? I don't have a left arm, and that guy could have seriously injured me. Besides, you only taught me to master one move. What made you think I could win with only one move?'

"'There is only one defense for that move,' the instructor said, 'and that is for your opponent to grab your left arm.'

"Do you get the message?" Mr. Christopher asked the players. "The instructor had taught the boy to believe in the process. Tomorrow night, it won't be the process that beats you. It will be self-doubt. Believe in yourself and your teammates. This is what has been missing with this team. This is what has caused Lincoln's current losing streak. Believe you will win. Believe in each other. Get rid of your doubts."

"That's right boys," Coach Morris interjected, catching on to the excitement. "You can't win football games if you don't think you can win."

"Satchel Paige, the old great baseball player in the Negro

leagues, never knew how old he was," Mr. Christopher told the boys. "Everyone knew that Satchel had to be up in years because he'd been pitching for so long. Old Satch just kept playing and playing. One day, determined to know his age, a group of reporters surrounded him and asked, 'Satch, how old are you?'

"Satchel replied, 'If you didn't know how old you were, how old would you be?'

"I pose this question to you: What kind of Lincoln team would suit up for tomorrow's game if you had no preconceptions about yourselves?"

Coach Morris scanned the eyes of his team and saw a confidence shining from them that he hadn't seen in a long time.

"Two railroad workers were sitting on a bench," Mr. Christopher continued. "The president of the company walked by and stopped to say hello to one of them. Afterward, the other worker said to his friend, 'I'm impressed. How did you become such good buddies with the president?'

"'He and I started for the railroad at the same time. We worked side by side doing manual labor,' the worker answered.

"'But he's the president, and you're still a laborer.'

"'Yes, I know,' he sighed. 'I came to work to earn $1.40 an hour, and he came to work to build a railroad.'

"You see, it's all up here in your head," Mr. Christopher said, pointing to his forehead. "Envision yourself as a superior athlete playing on an unbeatable team. A winning team runs like a well-tuned precision machine with each player executing his job with perfection. If you work together, each of you doing exactly what you're supposed to do, you'll be a winning football team. Together, this is how you can beat Jacktown."

Mr. Christopher stopped to let the message sink in. There was complete silence in the room. He paced back and forth. Raising his voice a notch, he continued.

"There was a man on a bicycle on a high wire above Niagara Falls. After he crossed from one side of the falls to the other side, he took off the tire and rode across on the rims only. The crowd cheered.

"'I'm going to do it again,' he told the audience, 'but this time, I want a volunteer to ride on the handlebars. Who wants to volunteer?'

"No hands went up. Everyone was silent. A little girl raised her hand. 'I'll go with you.'

"The man placed her on the handlebars and the people started to scream, 'Don't do it. She's only a child. How could you be so hardhearted? Stop.'

"The man ignored their cries and rode across the falls, turned around, and started to come back. On his return trip, there were loud cheers. He was a hero.

"Several reporters rushed to interview the man and the small girl. One asked her, 'Why would you do that? You could have been killed.'

"'He's my father,' she answered, 'and I trust him.'

"The trust of a child. It's been said that to enter the gates of heaven, you must come with the trust of a child."

There was a calm silence in the room. Nobody seemed to move. It was almost as if time were standing still.

"Two brothers, Albrecht and Albert Dürer, lived in a small village near Nuremberg, Germany, in the late fifteenth century," Mr. Christopher said in a voice barely above a whisper.

"The Dürer family was poor and had eighteen children. The father, a goldsmith, worked eighteen-hour days in his constant struggle to put food on the table for his large family. The two oldest sons, Albrecht and Albert, had a dream. They both wanted to pursue their talent for art. To fulfill their dream, they'd have to study at the Art Academy in Nuremberg. The two boys made a pact. They'd toss a coin, and the loser would labor in the local coalmines, and with his earnings, he'd pay his brother's way to attend the academy. Four years later, after finishing his art studies, it would then be the winner's turn to support his brother so he could study art at the academy. Albrecht won the toss and went to Nuremberg to become an artist. Meanwhile, Albert went down into the hazardous mines."

The boys leaned in, not wanting to miss a word.

"At the art academy, Albrecht was immediately recognized as a gifted artist. Upon his graduation, he was paid big fees for his commissioned works. His family held a festive dinner to celebrate his graduation on the lawn of their meager home. Albrecht made a toast to Albert: 'This is for you, dear brother, because you sacrificed for me and worked in the mines. Now it's my turn to take care of you, and you shall pursue your dream. It is your turn to attend the art academy.'

"Albert stood up and with tears streaming down his cheeks, he said, 'I am so proud and happy for you, my brother, but I am afraid it is too late for me. All of my fingers are broken, twisted, bent, and arthritic. As you can see, I can't even return your toast because I can't pick up this glass, let alone a paint brush.'

"Albrecht Dürer became one of the most famous artists of his time, and today his work appears in museums all over the world. As a tribute to his brother, he painted his brother's busted hands with palms together and thin fingers extended skyward. He called his drawing, *Hands*. This great masterpiece has since been renamed, *The Praying Hands*. Millions of reproductions have been distributed around the world, and I'm sure you're familiar with this famous work of art. The next time you see a copy, think about the story behind it and remember, 'Nobody makes it alone.'"

"We've got a pair of those praying hands on our living room wall," one of the boys spoke out. "Yeah, so do we," said another.

"We need each other. You must go into this game and encourage each other. Yes, there are going to be some tough spots. This is going to be a tough game. Expect it. They are going to be a great team. But you will be a great team too. You will win one play at a time. You have to expect them to bring all they've got. And likewise, you will bring all you've got!

"You must go out there thinking, *My opponent is going to be unbelievable—every single play. I am going to line up against him, and I am going to bring the best of me.* Do that, and the scoreboard and the final score will take care of itself. Repeat to yourself, *I will bring the best of me, EVERY SINGLE PLAY*. Don't look at the scoreboard. Just focus on your assignment, one play at a time. Again, the scoreboard and the final score will take care of itself."

"That's right," Coach Morris echoed in a husky voice. "The scoreboard and the final score will take care of itself."

"St. Peter asked a group of mice in heaven, 'How do you like it up here?' Mr. Christopher said.

I WILL BRING THE BEST OF ME, EVERY SINGLE PLAY.

"'We like it, but heaven is so big,' one mouse answered.

"'Yeah, the place is so spread out that we really don't get to see much of it,' another mouse volunteered.

"'Could you give each of us a pair of roller skates so we can get around easier in heaven?' one of the mice asked.

"St. Peter said that he would, and each mouse received a pair of skates.

"A few days later, St. Peter went back to check on the mice, but he couldn't find them. He did, however, come across a very big, fat, lazy cat that had been taking a snooze. St. Peter asked the cat the same question: 'How do you like it up here?'

"The cat said, 'It's wonderful. The streets are lined with

gold. The sun shines all the time. It's beautiful. And do you know what I like the most? I love those meals on wheels.'"

This time everyone in the room laughed. Mr. Christopher held up the football, the laughter stopped, and he continued.

"There's not going to be any meals on wheels tomorrow. You can be sure that nothing is going to be easy. Expect the player aligned across from you to be the best you've ever gone up against. Expect him to be the toughest you've ever seen. But do you know what? He's going to be up against the toughest opponent that he's ever faced. I don't want anyone to panic. I don't want anyone to be a grasshopper. I want you to be steady. I want you to do your best every play! That's right. Focus on every play, one play at a time. And each time, do your best."

Mr. Christopher reached in his jacket pocket. He held an object in his hand above his head. "Can you all see this steel-cast replica of the Lincoln High School stadium I'm holding in my hand? In 1961 the River Steel Corporation made thousands of them to commemorate the company's fiftieth anniversary. I bet many of your folks have one of them on display in your house. Raise your hand if your family has one."

Hands shot up in the air.

"Wow. I'm guessing nearly every household in Lincoln must have one."

Hands were lowered and he continued. "Well, tomorrow night, this stadium is going to be filled to capacity. All 9,500 seats will be sold, and there will be a lot more people standing. According to the *Lincoln Gazette*, most of the local fans are coming to see what has been heralded as the greatest high school football team ever in the state of Ohio. That's right. They're coming so they can say they saw the incredible Jacktown team of 1975, a team that will be talked about for decades to come.

"Now there is nothing any of you can do about what all those fans are thinking. You can't control what's going on in their minds. But what you can control is what happens on a small patch of land inside this stadium. That patch of land is 100 yards long and just a shade more than 53 yards wide. I want you all to stay focused on what you do on the playing field. This is the only thing that matters tomorrow night. And of course you can control what's going on in your mind. To do that, you must focus on one play at a time.

YOU CAN CONTROL WHAT'S GOING ON IN YOUR MIND.

"To beat Jacktown, everyone must be totally focused on executing his job. Now, you offensive linemen—each of you has an assignment, and that's to master the box. The box that I refer to is a three-by-three-foot area around you. That's your territory when you face your opponent on the line. Your sole job is to keep him from getting past this small area of turf. On every offensive play, you will engage in a battle to defend your turf, to block your opposing lineman—if he gets past you, you lose; if he doesn't get past you, you win. This is your one and only responsibility. Remember now, all five of you offensive linemen must work together with each of you controlling his three-by-three-foot turf. Do this, and Lincoln will control the line. When you take control of the line, you greatly enhance the chances of a successful run, pass, or kick. In tomorrow's game, your teammates are expecting you to master *your* box. They trust you will do this for them. You're not going to let them down, are you?"

This time he threw the ball to a stocky red-headed kid in the front row.

"What are you going to do, Rodney?"

Rodney Keller, an offensive guard, stood up and shouted, "I'm going to master my box, sir." Following his lead, three other linemen stood up and yelled, "I'm going to master my box."

The football was returned to Mr. Christopher, and he continued. "I am certain that everyone in this room is familiar with John F. Kennedy's famous quotation, 'Ask not what your country can do for you; ask what you can do for your country.' I want each of you to ask yourself, 'What can I give to the other people in this room?' These are your teammates. You don't want to let them down. This is why you're going to play your peak performance on every down. You are doing it for them. Now if everyone does his best each and every play, Lincoln will play its finest game ever.

"In one of his most famous speeches, the Reverend Martin

Luther King Jr. said to his audience, 'If you are a street cleaner, you should sweep the streets in such a way that the angels in heaven will stop, look down, and say, 'There goes a great street cleaner.'[11] I want the angels in heaven to look down at tomorrow's game and say the same about each of you: 'There goes a great football player.'"

Coach Morris studied the expressions on his players' faces and noticed that some of them were mouthing the words, "There goes a great player." Morris had never witnessed such a reaction by a football squad. *This is amazing*, he thought to himself.

"Mohandas Gandhi quoted the teachings from the classic Indian book *Bhagavad Gita*," Mr. Christopher told the team. "Throughout the book is the reference to the Buddhist and Hindu word *dharma*. It loosely translates in English to mean that everything is what it is due to nature. A parable in the book tells about a holy man who rescues a drowning scorpion in a pond. The holy man lifts the scorpion out of the water, and it stings him. The sting causes the man to drop the scorpion, and it falls into the water. Again, the holy man picks it up, and once more he is stung, and again he drops it. This happens several times.

"A passing farmer happens to be watching and finally inquires, 'Why do you keep on rescuing the scorpion when every time you do, he keeps stinging you?'

"The holy man answers, 'Because the dharma of the scorpion is to sting. It is what a scorpion does.'

"'But why do you keep saving it?'

"'Because it is my dharma to rescue it from distress, or in this case, a certain death by drowning. It is what I do,' the holy man replied.

"This parable illustrates the meaning of dharma. And tomorrow, I want each of you to do what you're expected to do. I want you to be totally focused on every play of the game. Do that, and you'll do your best. You each have an assignment to do on every play, and I want you to do it to the best of your ability. Why? BECAUSE THIS IS WHAT YOU DO!"

"This is what I do," rippled quietly across the locker room as several of the players chanted in barely audible voices.

"A while ago, my lawn was in such bad shape that I called a lawn-care service to treat it," Mr. Christopher said. "The next day, a company rep came to my home, took a quick look at my lawn, and said it was beyond help. 'Nothing we could do for it, sir,' and the man got back in his truck and drove away. Now I've faced rejection before in my life, but this was the first time I was ever rejected by a lawn-care company. My neighbor has a nice yard, and I knew he grew up on a farm, so I asked him for his advice.

"'Don't worry about that guy,' he said 'Just keep planting grass.'

"'What about all the weeds?' I asked.

"'Don't pull any weeds. Just keep planting grass. And be patient.'

"I did what he instructed me to do. I kept planting grass

and paid no attention to the weeds. It took a while, but today, the grass on my lawn is beautiful.

"You see, it's about having a process and consistency. Coach Morris has a process for you to follow. He's had one all season. Now you have to be consistent—you have to execute it. This means each and every one of you. One play at a time. Everyone plays his best. Another thing: you've got to trust each other. This is a game about trust. Nobody lets the team down. Everyone does his job. Just keep planting grass. This is how football games are won. To beat Jacktown, it will require an entire team effort. Is this clear to everyone? Raise your hand in the air if you understand what I've just told you."

Mr. Christopher raised the football in the air, and every player raised his hand.

"If there is one thing I can assure you, it is that you will have adversity on the field tomorrow. Football is a game about adversity. In every play, players get knocked down, they get back up, and then they get knocked down again. But you keep getting up. Having adversity is part of the game. You accept it, but you don't allow it to defeat you. You go on to the next play. So when one of your teammates faces adversity in the game, each of you must have one thought—you are the one who will be there for him. Know that you will stay focused on the process during the entire game, and part of the process is being there for each other. Let every one of your teammates know that he can trust you to do your job. As your teammate, he can trust you on every play—one play at a time. This is how football games are won. One play at a time! Now, I want you to all stand up again and tell one of your teammates how much you trust him and listen to him tell you how much he trusts you. And be sure to promise him that you won't let him down in the game tomorrow night."

The whole team stood up, and again they talked one-on-one to each other. Mr. Christopher let them talk for about two minutes. He raised the football above his head, then the talking stopped and everyone sat down.

HAVING ADVERSITY IS PART OF THE GAME. YOU ACCEPT IT, BUT YOU DON'T ALLOW IT TO DEFEAT YOU.

"During the *Apollo 13* voyage," Mr. Christopher said, "an explosion caused the shuttle to lose both fuel and oxygen on the return to Earth. Mission Captain Jim Lovell calmly said to mission control on Earth: 'Houston, we've had a problem here.'

"There was indeed a serious problem. An onboard explosion caused malfunctions that strongly reduced the chances of the astronauts safely returning. Instead of panicking, Lovell assumed his role on the mission—making sure he and his crew returned safely. He took immediate charge of the situation. It didn't take a rush of adrenaline to shoot through his entire body for him to know that the space capsule was in serious danger. Lovell ignored all distraction, and he focused only on what he must do so everyone would survive. He went right to the process—Lovell trusted the fact that if he stayed fully focused on the process, they would return home safely. Tomorrow, you will focus on one play at a time. And you will trust that this will assure you of a positive outcome."

Mr. Christopher paused briefly and walked to the center of the room. "There is another lesson to be learned from the *Apollo 13* voyage," he continued. "And that's to remember that things don't always run smoothly. There are so many variables in an undertaking like the returning of a spaceship that you must be prepared for the unexpected to happen. This is true in all endeavors, including a football game. In tomorrow's game, you will make mistakes and at times, your opponent will excel. Expect it, and when it happens, don't be discouraged. Forget about the last play, and focus on the current play. And when things aren't going your way, do not allow yourself to become discouraged."

Mr. Christopher threw the ball to Johnny Corleone.

"You're the quarterback, Johnny. I want you to tell your teammates what you're going to do if you get sacked or throw an interception."

Corleone, an attractive, lanky boy, stood up. Although he looked athletic, his slight build seemed more suited for a basketball court than the football field. Even so, he spoke with a quiet confidence, and from the reaction of the other players, he was clearly a team leader. "It's only one play," he said, carefully choosing his words, "and I'm not going to let it get to me. I'll tell myself that I will do better next time."

"Very good, Johnny," Mr. Christopher nodded approvingly.

"Winston Churchill was once asked to deliver a commencement speech to the boys of an old private school," he continued, "and his message was memorable for both its truth and its brevity. The great British prime minister approached the podium, faced his audience and said: 'This is the lesson: never give in, never give in—never, never, never, never, in nothing great or small, large or petty, never give in except to convictions of honour and good sense. Never yield to force; never yield to the apparently overwhelming might of the enemy.'

NEVER GIVE IN, NEVER GIVE IN, NEVER, NEVER, NEVER . . .

"Having said these few words, Churchill walked away from the podium. It's probable that nobody in the audience ever forgot his message. He could have spoken for an hour and not have had such an impact.

"This afternoon I repeat, 'Never, never, never give in.' There will be times when you are down in tomorrow's game, but you must never succumb to defeat. Remember that nobody—not one man in this room—gives in tomorrow night. You play as a team, and you win as a team.

"Never, never give in," Corleone repeated for all to hear.

"A mother was worried about her small son who was late coming home from school," Mr. Christopher said. "When the little boy finally walked in the door, she anxiously said to him, 'Where have you been? I was worried sick about you.'

"'There was another little boy and his bicycle was broke,' he told her, 'so I had to help him.'

"'Hey, wait a minute, young man,' she said. 'You don't know anything about fixing bicycles.'

"'I know,' the little boy answered. 'I had to sit down and help him cry.'

"Tomorrow, you're all going to be there for each other. You are going to help each other. You are going to be focused all together."

Mr. Christopher paused. There was a hush in the room as everyone waited to hear what the stranger would say next.

"A friend of mine once told me about his boyhood, reflecting on how he remembered his father. As a little boy, after returning home from the grocery store with his father, he had a comic book in his pocket.

"'Where did you get that?' the father asked.

"'I took it from the grocery store.'

"The father expressed his disappointment and went back to the store to pay for it. A week later, the boy came home with another comic book from the grocery store. When the father saw it, he asked, "Where did you get that?" The boy told him, and again, the father said that is wrong to steal, and he went back to the store and paid for it.

"A third time, the boy stole another comic book, and this time the father put the boy over his knee and spanked him. It was the first and only time he had ever struck his son, my friend told me.

"'That was the last time I ever stole anything,' my friend explained.

"'So by getting spanked you learned a good lesson and that's what stopped you from stealing?' I asked.

"'No. What stopped me was afterward,' my friend said. 'Hearing my father cry outside my room in the hallway—that's what stopped me.'

"I think there's a good moral here about caring and trusting. Knowing that your teammates care about you and trust you is what matters in tomorrow's game. It's also about how you care about them and how you trust them. You must trust all of your teammates. Everyone here contributes to the end result. If you don't trust each other, you don't trust anyone."

Mr. Christopher tossed the ball to Mark Mitchell, who was sitting in the center of the room. While not particularly big, Mitchell was strong.

"Good catch, Mitch," the speaker said. "Of course, you're a linebacker so you're expected to stay focused on the ball— and by the way, it's okay if you catch a few tomorrow night. Now what does trust mean to you?"

I WILL DO MY BEST TO LIVE UP
TO THEIR EXPECTATIONS.

Mitchell stood up and said, "Sir, I know my teammates trust me to play my best game ever. And that's exactly what I'm going to do. Knowing that they trust me means that I can't let them down—I will do my best to live up to their expectations. That's a promise, sir."

Mitchell passed the football back. Mr. Christopher looked Mitchell in the eye and nodded his head in approval. "I have full confidence in you, son." He then continued. "I'm reminded about another little boy who was upset with his parents and ran away from home. He packed two cans of root beer, two Twinkies, and went to the park. He sat down on a park bench next to an old woman to have one of his Twinkies and a root beer. He offered her a Twinkie, and she accepted it. Then he gave his other root beer to her, and she took it too. After he finished, he decided to go home and walked away. He took a few steps, turned around, walked back to the old woman and gave her a hug. She gave him a warm smile.

"When the little boy returned home, his mother asked him about his day and why he was so happy. 'I just met God in the park,' he answered, 'and she had the most beautiful smile.'

"The elderly woman went home and her son asked her about her day and why she was so happy. 'I just met God in the park,' she answered, 'and He's a lot younger than I thought He would be.'"

Coach Morris studied the players' faces and was surprised to see a few tears. He saw a lineman put his arms in the air as if to yawn, and as he lowered his right arm, he wiped his eyes. *This Mr. Christopher is really good*, the coach thought to himself.

"The story about the small boy and elderly woman is about love. In John 15:12, Jesus said, 'This is my commandment, that you love one another as I have loved you.' Note that Jesus didn't suggest or ask us to love each other. He commanded it. I want all of you to love each other. Because when you love another person, you want to do your best for him. You also trust that person. Trust every man on this team and believe that he will do his job on Friday night."

"Trust," Morris said in a loud voice for emphasis. Many of the players responded by repeating the word, "Trust."

"Winning in life is about caring for other people and believing in them," Mr. Christopher went on. "You have to believe in the process in tomorrow's game. You must have trust. You have to trust that Coach Morris will make the right decisions on which players are put into the game and what plays are called. You have to trust each other. You must trust that each of your teammates will do his assignment on every play—just like you will do yours for them. Trust that nobody will let you or the team down. Believe in each other. You trust because you care about each other. Remember that. Now why do you trust each other?"

"Because we care about each other," the team shouted.

"Yes, you care for each other, and because you love each other."

"Yes, because we love each other," Corleone shouted.

Mr. Christopher went on. "In Mark 11:24, we are told: 'Whatever you ask for in prayer, believe that you have received it, and it will be yours.'

"I want you to believe that Lincoln will beat Jacktown tomorrow night. I want you to paint a vivid picture in your mind that Lincoln has won the game. Visualize what you must do in every play to make it happen. Ask for it, believe in it, and it will happen."

Mr. Christopher stopped to let the players digest what he said. Pacing back and forth, he then said, "There is a story about the late Martin Luther King Jr., who was sitting in the back of the bus and saying to himself: 'I may walk to the back of the bus, but I left my mind in the front of the bus. One day I am going to put my body up there where my mind is.'

"Do you see what belief and prayer can accomplish? Rather than feeling bitter and resentful, Dr. King pictured a positive thought. It was an image of what he visualized would be in the future and a vision that he asked for in prayer. Then he worked to make his prayer come true."

Mr. Christopher held the football high above his head and waited again for complete silence. He then said, "I'll wrap this up now by asking each of you to say a prayer tonight before you go to sleep. In your prayer, ask God that you and all of your teammates play to the best of your abilities. Tell God how much you trust every one of them, and ask Him to help you be focused on every play. Also pray that nobody, including your opponents, is injured in the game. Do this, and believe in your prayer. What you ask for will be yours.

"God bless you."

A solemn quiet filled the room. Unlike previous pep talks, nobody applauded. Nor were there any high fives. In fact, nobody said a word for several long minutes. Finally Coach Morris broke the silence. "Okay, guys, that's it for tonight. Remember now, lights off by 9:30; I want you all to get a good night's sleep so you'll be well rested for tomorrow's game."

After the last player had left, Coach Morris asked an assistant, "I'm looking for Mr. Christopher. Have you seen him anywhere?"

"Say, who was he? And how did he know all the players' names?" the assistant coach asked.

"I'll be sure to ask him that when I talk to him," Morris answered. "Where is he?"

"He took off immediately after he finished speaking," the assistant coach answered. "Sure seemed in a hurry."

THE LINCOLN-
JACKTOWN GAME

Driving on the interstate, Mr. Christopher turned the dial on his radio and tuned into the game. He glanced skyward and said, "It's showtime."

"It's standing room only here in Lincoln, Ohio," the voice on the radio said. "This is a 9,500-seat stadium, but there must be 12,000 fans here tonight. This crowd brings back memories from the '50s, when the Lions were a real powerhouse. That's when Jack Morris was Lincoln's great running back. Mr. Reliable, Number 13. Here's a bit of trivia, sports fans: Guess whose number is the only one ever retired by Lincoln High School? Yes, that's right, folks, Jack Morris's number, the same Jack Morris who is Lincoln's present head coach. The way the team has been losing games, though, this could very well be his last season. I understand he sells real estate in the off-season. Don't give up your part-time sales job, Jack.

"The visiting team has strutted onto the field. Boy, they look big. The crowd is giving them a standing ovation. It's been this way all season. The Giants are getting the respect that's due them. They are undoubtedly one of the greatest high school teams in Ohio history. Certainly the best this announcer has ever seen.

"Now here comes the Lincoln Lions . . . I don't believe it; the crowd barely stirred. Some fans are cheering them on, but nothing like what we just heard when the Giants came out—I'm even hearing some booing. Now, that's just not right. I don't care how many games the Lions have lost. They are the hometown team, and let's not forget, they're high school kids. I am really disappointed in the poor sportsmanship just exhibited by these fans. It's just not called for. After this announcement, I'll be back with the kickoff."

The band played "The Star-Spangled Banner," and after the coin toss the announcer said, "Lincoln won the toss and has elected to kick. I don't get it. If I were Coach Morris, I'd want to keep the ball out of the Giants' hands. Especially their great running back, Billy Thomas—he definitely gets my vote for this year's Mr. Football in Ohio. He has twenty-one touchdowns and 1,865 rushing yards. Now that's what I call a lot of real estate, sports fans.

"Number 1, Josh Goldman, is the Lions' place kicker. He kicks the ball and it's caught by Billy Thomas on the 20. There is a swarm of blue uniforms around the speedster at the 30. I see one missed tackle, two, no make that three missed tackles. Thomas breaks through, and he's in the open. And nobody is going to catch him. Man, that boy can fly. He's at the 30, the 20, the 10—touchdown. We're ten seconds into this game and it's Jacktown, 6; Lincoln, zip. This crowd is awestruck. They came to see the best team in the land, and they will not be denied. No doubt about it. Billy Thomas has to be the best running back in high school football. I'll put him up against anyone. Yes sir, anyone. You can be sure there are college scouts in the stands every time Jacktown takes the field—wait one second, folks. A flag is on the field. The referee is indicating that the Giants were offside on the kickoff. They're calling the touchdown back. Lincoln will kick again from their 45-yard line. We'll pause for a commercial."

"Yes," said Mr. Christopher, blocking out a commercial. "Go Lions."

"Josh Goldman kicks the ball, but it's off the side of his foot. The ball takes a bounce on the Jacktown 40-yard line," the announcer says. "A terrible kick. The ball is loose. There is a swarm of players with both red and blue jerseys around the ball. And wait . . . the blue team has come up with the ball! How about this one, sports fans? Josh Goldman has recovered his own kick! The Lions have the ball on the Jacktown 38-yard line. Somebody up there must like the Lions. You don't very often see the place kicker muff the ball and then recover it. But as the saying goes, folks, that's the way the ball bounces.

"Johnny Corleone takes the snap and throws a bullet pass to his tight end. It's caught and the Lions have the ball on the 26-yard line. First down for Lincoln."

Three running plays moved the ball to the 18-yard line. "It's fourth and 2 yards for the Lions, and Josh Goldman is in to attempt the field goal. He has made four in eighteen attempts this season, his longest only 21 yards. This will be a 34-yard kick. The ball is snapped, it's in the air . . . it's good! Lincoln gets on the board first. How about that! We're three minutes into this game and Lincoln is beating Jacktown, 3–0. The Giants don't appear to be the least bit worried, folks. In fact, I think the Lions might have just made them mad. Believe me on this one—the last thing you want to do is fire up a team the likes of Jacktown."

On the kickoff, the ball was caught on the 20-yard line by Jimmy Sims and was returned to the 40-yard line. "The Giants will start on their own 40 with good field position," said the announcer. "If you just tuned in, we're only minutes into this game, and it's 3 to zip in favor of the Lions. That's right, folks, you heard it right. It's Lincoln, 3; Jacktown, 0.

"First and 10, and the ball is handed to Billy Thomas. He takes the ball off right tackle and is down in Lions' territory on the 46-yard line. An easy first down for the Giants.

"Okay, it's first and 10 on the 46. Tony Scala takes the snap and throws a quick pass just over the center of the line, and it is knocked down by Mark Mitchell. Good defensive play for the Lions' linebacker. The Giants break the huddle, line up, and Scala throws a pass to his tight end. It's a completion, and Jacktown has the ball at the 33-yard line. First and 10.

"The Giants try a reverse with Scala handing the ball off to

Sammy Pittman. He's hit by linebacker Mark Mitchell for a 6-yard loss. That's two excellent defensive plays for Mitchell in this drive.

"The Giants start on the 39-yard line. The ball is given to Billy Thomas who carries it to the 29-yard line, a pick up of ten for the sensational halfback. It's third and 6, and Thomas again gets the ball; he cuts wide around the left side of the line, and he picks up five more yards.

"It's fourth and 1 on the 24-yard line, and there's no question the Giants will go for it. The ball is snapped, and Scala runs into a wall of blue. He goes nowhere. The Lions stopped him cold, and they take over on their own 24-yard line. Can you believe it? This home-team crowd likes what they see. The fans give a big applause for the defensive unit as they walk off the field. I can see Coach Morris down there, high-fiving his defensive players on the sidelines."

On the next series, the Lions ran a mix of passing and running plays. Quarterback Johnny Corleone completed four out of seven passes, and Lincoln moved the ball to Jacktown's 38-yard line. It's fourth down, 2 yards.

"They're bringing in Josh Goldman to punt," the announcer says. "The ball is snapped, and Goldman punts a high kick that bounces on the 11-yard line. Blue uniforms swarm around the ball; it's rolling, rolling, and it stops on the one-yard line where Lincoln downs it. It's first and 10 on the 1-yard line for the Giants. Who would have ever imagined? We'll be back after a message from our sponsors."

Mr. Christopher chuckled as he drove through the night with the radio on full blast. "Stay focused, Lions. Believe in yourselves. Trust each other."

STAY FOCUSED.

On the first play, Pittman carried the ball up center for a 1-yard gain. The next play, Thomas was stopped on the 4-yard line by Mark Mitchell. On third down, Giants quarterback, Tony Scala, threw a pass that was caught and dropped as a result of a hard hit by Mitchell. The Giants were forced to kick from their end zone on fourth down. Lincoln took over on the 44-yard line. "Lincoln has great field position, and there's no doubt about it, folks, the Lions are in this ball game, late in the first quarter. By George, they're even ahead."

On the next series, Johnny Corleone completed five passes, picking up three first downs, with the ball ending up on the Jacktown 4-yard line. The next three plays were two runs that failed to produce any yardage and a missed pass in the end zone. "That one was nearly picked off by the Giants," the announcer said, "and had he made the catch, he would have gone the distance untouched. It's now fourth down, four seconds on the clock in the first quarter, and Josh Goldman is coming in to attempt the field goal. I remind you, folks, that the Giants have blocked nine this season, a state record. Here's the snap, the Giants are charging. Goldman gets the kick up in the air, and . . . it's good! The Lions lead 6 to 0! Listen to that crowd! They're really into this game now. The first quarter has ended, and the Lions are on top. Six to zip. We'll be right back."

Both teams moved the ball up and down the field in the second quarter, but there were no points put on the board. With twenty-six seconds left on the clock before the half, Scala completed a 50-yard pass to Sammy Pittman who was forced out of bounds on the 9-yard line. Billy Thomas ran up the middle for 2 yards, and the Giants called a time-out with fifteen seconds remaining on the clock. The Giants lined up quickly and threw a pass, but it was knocked down by Mark Mitchell in the end zone. On third down, Scala tried a quarterback sneak and was stopped on the 1-yard line. The Giants called a time-out to stop the clock.

"It's fourth down, and Jacktown is behind 6–0," the announcer said. "With three seconds left in the first half, the Giants have the ball on the 1-yard line. *Keep in mind they haven't been shut out for an entire half all season.* Scala gets the ball, he hands off to Thomas. A big hole in the line opens on the right side, and he scores. The score is tied 6–6." The Giants made the extra point and they were ahead 7–6 at the half.

"Lincoln has managed to stay in this ballgame," the announcer said. "The Giants lead by one point. It's been a long time since any team has challenged them like this. The question is, can Lincoln keep it up? The Giants have outscored their opponents by 26 points in the second half. They are big, and they are strong. They are a well-disciplined team and in excellent physical condition. Will they wear down the smaller Lincoln Lions during the second half? It's highly probable. But you've got to give credit to the Lions and their head coach, Jack Morris, for putting up a terrific first half. And how about their quarterback, Johnny Corleone, with eleven completions in seventeen attempts? Throughout the entire 1975 season, no quarterback has had ten completions against Jacktown. And what's more impressive is that Corleone has only been sacked once. Considering how much they are outsized by the Giants, Lincoln's offensive line is holding up quite well.

"And on the other side of the ball (is the fact that) linebacker Mark Mitchell has twelve tackles, two sacks, and he's broken up five passes. What a first half for Mitchell! The guy averages four tackles a game! And what about that Number 1, Josh Goldman? Not only does he have two field goals, he recovered his own kickoff that set up the Lions' first score.

"The big question is, can the Lions keep up this performance in the second half against the Jacktown Giants, a team that's undefeated in their last forty-one games, and a three-time state champion? Can the winless Lincoln Lions continue to play with the same level of intensity for the entire game? Remember now, it was just last Friday night when a weak Middleburg shut out the Lions 28–0. I guarantee one thing—the entire stadium here in Lincoln is wondering what on earth Coach Jack Morris did to get his team so fired up . . . Well, don't go away, folks. It looks as if we might just have ourselves a good old-fashioned barnburner here tonight in Lincoln, Ohio."

Driving down the interstate, a revved-up Mr. Christopher said, "Okay, Coach, there are still two quarters left in this game," just as if he were in the locker room talking to Jack Morris. "Tell your boys that the Jacktown Giants are not giants after all. You're right in this game. Let them know how well they're doing and since they stayed with Jacktown for the first half, they can do it again for the next half. Let your team know that they can win it. Remind them to stay focused. Forget about the scoreboard. Every man executes his assignment, and everyone trusts that each of his teammates will do his job. Trust. Believe in each other. Tell your offensive linemen to master their box. Just keep on planting grass. Everyone plays his best game. You win one play at a time. Tell them what we are told in Mark 11:24, 'Whatever you ask for in prayer, believe that you have received it, and it will be yours.' And one more thing, Coach, have them say a prayer before the start of the second half."

Meanwhile, in the locker room, the players' heads were down while each boy said a silent prayer.

"Okay, guys," Coach Morris said, "let's go out and do even better for the next half of the game. We've proven that we are a worthy opponent, and the Jacktown team knows they're up against a formidable foe. Remember: stay focused and forget about the scoreboard. It's one play at a time. I want each of you to do his job. And trust that your teammates will do theirs. Let's do it!"

The fired-up Lions ran onto the field to a standing ovation, a hardy welcome that a Lincoln team had not received for many years.

"Both teams are back on the field for the second half of this exciting game," the announcer said. "The score is 7–6. The powerful Jacktown Giants are up by a single point. The tenacious Lions are putting up a ferocious fight. Nobody in this state predicted such a close game. But we still have two more quarters of football to play, and as we know, the Jacktown Giants know how to put points on the scoreboard in the second half. The second half is about to start. We'll find out."

Mr. Christopher listened intently to the whistle signaling the second half of play, but then his radio began to pick up a lot of static. He found a new station just in time to pick up the beginning of the half.

"There's the kickoff, and Vinny Tarantino takes it on the 15-yard line. He runs up the center, he breaks one tackle, and he's hit on the 30-yard line. The Lions are off to a good start in this second half, folks."

The Lincoln team made two first downs, but after moving into Jacktown territory were forced to punt from the 42-yard line. Josh Goldman punted a high spiraling kick, and Billy Thomas signaled for a fair catch on the 10-yard line.

"The Jacktown offense takes the field for the first time in

this second half," the announcer said. "Remember, this is a disciplined, well-conditioned football team. Frankly, I don't see how Lincoln can hold them at bay. These Giants are simply too good a ball team."

Static on Mr. Christopher's radio once again drowned out the announcer. He turned the dial, switching from station to station, but could no longer pick up the game. "Remember boys," he muttered to himself. "Trust. One play at a time. Master the box. Believe in yourselves. You are not grasshoppers. You can do it."

A while later, Mr. Christopher had driven to the outskirts of Cleveland, where he tried again—this time successfully—to pick up the game on his radio. "This is WHHO-AM broadcasting what will be forevermore known here in Lincoln as 'The Game.' Folks, this is Ohio high school football in its finest hour. There are forty-two seconds remaining on the clock and Lincoln is backed up deep in its own territory. The ball is on the 12-yard line. The clock is stopped with an incompleted pass. The score remains 7–6, and the Lions have one time-out remaining. It's fourth down and the Lions are going for it. Jack Morris sends the play. Corleone goes back into the pocket near his end zone. He's being blitzed and he throws a quick pass to the sidelines that's . . . caught by Vinny Tarantino! Tarantino races down the sidelines. There's nobody near him! He's still going, going, and he crosses into Jacktown territory. Here comes one player, Ricky Jones, to stop him. Jones forces Tarantino out of bounds at the 40-yard line. Thirty seconds remain on the clock! What an incredible offensive play under enormous pressure! That's number twenty for Johnny Corleone. What a record night he's having! He's twenty for twenty-eight. The crowd is on its feet going wild! No one has left this stadium tonight; in fact, it feels like more have come as the word of this possible upset spread!

"Okay, the Lions line up with Corleone in the shotgun. He receives the snap. He's under a lot of pressure. He throws the ball, and the pass is broken up on the 25-yard line. The clock shows twenty-one seconds remaining."

"Come on, Johnny," Mr. Christopher shouted. "You can do it."

"There's probably enough time for one, maybe two passes. A field goal will win this game, but they're not in field-goal territory. The ball is snapped and the blitz is on. Corleone can't find a receiver. He steps out of the pocket; nobody is open. He finds a hole in the center of the field. He keeps the ball. He breaks loose and is hit hard at the 30-yard line. The clock is down to three seconds as Lincoln calls its final time-out.

"Coach Morris is talking to his players. They're back on the field and Morris has sent in Josh Goldman to attempt the field goal. Goldman has two for the night, and this one will be from the 35-yard line, a 45-yard field-goal attempt. I'm told that Goldman has never kicked one from this distance in a game, not even in a practice. This one would put pressure on even Lou 'the Toe' Groza, the Browns' great kicker, perhaps the best the game has ever seen."

"You can do it, Josh," Mr. Christopher yelled out the window. "Come on, line. Don't let this one get blocked."

"What a game! Yes sir, we've got a real barnburner tonight," the announcer continued. "The ball is at the 30-yard line, and Goldman will attempt to kick it from the 35. There's a time-out on the field. Jacktown's last time-out. They want to ice Goldman. Now here's a kid who doesn't come into tonight's game with exactly what you'd call an impressive field-goal résumé. He's never made two field goals in a single game. Now he's going for his third field goal in this game and attempting the longest field goal of his life in the biggest game of his life. Talk about pressure. And Goldman, a senior, is barely seventeen years old. Okay, they're back on the field. Both teams line up and face each other on the 30. Here comes the snap. The ball is down, Goldman kicks it, and the ball is in the air. It's not a high kick, and it's going toward the right side of the goalpost. I don't know if it has enough power behind it . . . The ball hits the right side of the goalpost. It rebounds upward toward the left. It's good! It's good! Lincoln defeats the undefeated Giants, 9–7! What a game! What a win!

"Can you believe that Goldman did it? But, let me tell you folks, Goldman took a hard hit after the ball was in the air by Number 63, all-state 260-pound tackle Henry Greene. Greene just leveled him. There's a flag on the field for roughing the kicker, but Lincoln isn't about to take the penalty. This game is over. It's in the history books. We've just witnessed the biggest upset in Ohio high school football. You heard it right, folks. It's Lincoln, 9; Jacktown, 7. Jacktown's forty-one-game winning streak has ended. And oh yes, folks, so has Lincoln's twenty-four-game losing streak.

"This crowd is ecstatic. What a ballgame. I've never seen anything like it. The Lincoln Lions have just defeated the previously unbeaten Jacktown Giants. Yes, you heard that right folks. Lincoln, 9; Jacktown, 7.

"The fans have stormed the field. There is going to be a big celebration in Lincoln, Ohio, tonight. It will be a long time before they forget about this one."

After the Big Game and Whatever Happened to . . . ?

There was much joy in Lincoln, Ohio, after the Lions' big victory over the Jacktown Giants. A late-afternoon Saturday special edition of the *Lincoln Gazette* was dedicated to The Game. The headlines boldly stated: "LINCOLN WINS GREATEST FOOTBALL GAME EVER PLAYED." The subtitle was less overstated, claiming: "Lions Whip Giants in Colossal Upset."

Main articles embellished the individual Herculean athleticism, featuring Lincoln's three star performers. One article was titled: "Kicker Josh Goldman, Number 1, Outscores Jacktown with 9." Only a single sentence in the lengthy article mentioned that a late hit had caused Josh Goldman to suffer a broken femur in the last play of the game. A second article read in bold print: "Mark Mitchell: Breaks up 11 Passes, Has 24 Tackles." A third article heralded the quarterback; its title read: "Johnny Corleone Completes 20 out of 29." There was also a story about how three of the team's seniors had the game of their lives. The story's title read: "Lincoln Says Farewell to Three Courageous Lions: Corleone, Mitchell, and Goldman."

The *Lincoln Gazette* also praised Coach Jack Morris, old Mr. Reliable, who came through in the biggest game of his entire career—including his playing days in the '50s when he starred at Lincoln High School and later at Ohio State.

There had been a rumor that Coach Morris would be fired at the end of the year. After the Jacktown victory, nobody ever dared to bring up the subject of firing Jack Morris. His hero status had returned, and once again, he was the most popular man in Lincoln, Ohio. He continued to sell real estate during the summer months, and although he only worked at it part-time, he sold more real estate than any other agent in the entire county.

In February, Johnny Corleone broke his collarbone and right arm in a motorcycle accident and never played football again. Josh Goldman's leg healed, but he never again kicked another football. Mark Mitchell graduated and went to Ohio State where he majored in finance. He played intramural football for his fraternity.

In July 1976, after Johnny Corleone's graduation, the Corleone family moved to Toledo, where his father Tony Corleone got a job as a factory worker at the Jeep factory.

Josh's father, Harry Goldman, owner of Goldman's Clothiers,

a men's store on Main Street in downtown Lincoln, had become a victim of the community's hard times. After thirty-five years in business, Harry Goldman abruptly ran a going-out-of-business sale in August 1977 and closed his store forever. The GOB sale coincided with the expiration of his lease. That same year, the family moved to Cleveland Heights where Harry Goldman went to work for his brother-in-law who owned a wholesale food company.

After graduating from Ohio State as a finance major, Mark Mitchell took a job with State National Bank in Columbus, Ohio. After a series of acquisitions, State National became one of the largest regional banks in the United States. Having been on the bank's fast track and following a succession of promotions, Mark Mitchell was named CEO in 2001. His father, Bill Mitchell, a widower, remained in Lincoln where he worked as a self-employed house painter. In 1992, Bill Mitchell suffered a fatal heart attack.

Johnny Corleone went to Bowling Green State University in Bowling Green, Ohio, just forty miles south of Toledo, where he majored in engineering. After college he moved to Boston to work for a small technology company. Sometime later, along with two co-workers, he co-founded Alpha Technology. The company became hugely successful and was listed on the New York Stock Exchange. Johnny was later named chairman of the board and CEO.

Josh Goldman graduated from Wittenberg University in Springfield, Ohio, married his college sweetheart, and became a high school history teacher in Dayton, Ohio, his wife's hometown. He also coached the boy's soccer team.

During their youth in Lincoln, the three boys had only been casual friends and did not stay in touch after high school.

Pre-reunion

On the afternoon of Tuesday, September 28, 2003, John Corleone paced his plush office talking on his headset. "That's right, Bill, I'll be serving as the board chairman of the hospital concurrently with my remaining term as chair of the United Way board," the physically fit forty-four-year old executive said.

"You're the best," responded the voice on the other end of the phone. "When it comes to giving back to this community, I don't think I've ever heard you say no."

"Well, it's like we're told in Luke 12:48, Mayor," Corleone continued. "To whom much has been given, much will be required."

"And as I like to say, my good friend, if you want something done, you give it to a busy man. Have a great day, John."

"You too, Your Honor."

Upon hanging up, the voice on the intercom said, "Mr.

Corleone, I have a woman holding on line three. She wants to talk to Johnny Corleone. I've told her several times that you're tied up, but she said it's urgent and she'd wait. It's Margaret Morris."

"I don't recognize the name. Who's she with?"

"Said it was personal. Said to tell you she's Jack Morris's wife."

"I should have known," Corleone answered. "Nobody's called me Johnny since I left Lincoln. Talk about a name from the past. Yes, by all means put her through."

"Hello, Mrs. M," Corleone said. "I apologize for keeping you on hold."

"I was afraid you wouldn't remember who I was."

"It's been a long time, ma'am. Haven't seen you and Coach since my mom's funeral back in '89, a year after we lost my father. But sure I remember you. How are you and Coach Morris doing these days?"

"He's very sick, Johnny. Has a brain tumor, and the doctor says it's just a matter of time. Could be any day."

"Oh, I'm so sorry," Corleone replied. "You know it's been fifteen years since I've seen Coach. I still picture him as solid as a rock."

"Well Johnny, he's past seventy now and had been in great shape. Until recently, that is. Then he started getting these awful headaches about two years ago," Margaret Morris said in a soft voice. "He's been in and out of the Cleveland Clinic, and now they say there isn't anything they can do. We can only pray. Doctors say it's only a matter of a few weeks. Jack has requested that I call three of his former players. You, Josh Goldman, and Mark Mitchell. He would like you all to come here. Jack said he has to talk to you boys. I know it sounds dramatic, like one of those deathbed scenes you see in the movies. His exact words were, 'Tell the boys that it's urgent.'"

Margaret Morris's voice choked up; she struggled to continue. "We've been following your career, Johnny, and we're both so proud of you. Not only for your work, but your civic and charitable activities. And naturally we are aware of how busy you are."

"Is Coach lucid?"

"Not always. I'd have to say in and out. I can't even promise you that he'll be able to talk to you. But he's lucid now, and he insisted on me calling you."

"When does Coach want us all to be there?" Corleone interjected.

"I know this is on short notice, Johnny, but can you be here this Friday?" Margaret Morris whispered in a gentle hush.

"Hold on a sec, and I'll check," Johnny said, and facing his intercom he spoke out: "Katie, I need you to bring in my calendar so I can see what's on my agenda for Friday."

Katie Wilson, a heavy-set middle-aged executive assistant, entered the room. She handed a sheet of paper to her boss. "You have three committee meetings in the morning, you know, the usual ones, then lunch with Fred Benson, and at 2:00, the company helicopter is scheduled to take you to the Cape. You've got a mixed doubles tennis game with Liz and the Meyers at 4:30. On Saturday, you've got your regular golf game at the club at the Cape."

After glancing at his schedule, Corleone said, "Mrs. M, are you still there?"

"I'm here, Johnny, and I couldn't help hearing what your secretary was saying. Sounds like Friday won't work."

"What time would you like me to be there, Mrs. M?"

Margaret Morris said with a surprised ring in her voice, "If you could be here before noon on Friday."

"Will do, Mrs. M."

"Katie, do me a favor and cancel everything for this Friday," Corleone told his assistant. "I'll personally call Liz. Gosh, I hate to disappoint her. Oh yes, please tell Ted I'll need the company jet on Friday morning. Mrs. M, you still there? Good. Katie is getting on the line. Katie, please get the address, phone number, and directions to their house from Mrs. M."

The same afternoon, Mark Mitchell glanced momentarily at the name and phone number that his secretary left on his desk. All the while, he pensively studied the skyline of downtown Columbus from his spacious office on the top floor of the State National Bank building. The message had conjured up memories from his youth. It was a beautiful autumn day. *My favorite time of year and a perfect day for football*, he thought out loud as he dialed the number.

"Morris residence," answered a soft woman's voice.

"Mrs. M, This is Mitch—Mark Mitchell—returning your call. How are you?"

"Hey, there, Mitch, it's good to hear your voice."

"How's Coach Morris?"

"That's why I called. Not good. Coach has an inoperative brain tumor. Been in and out the last couple of weeks," Margaret Morris said, her voice cracking. "The doctor says that Coach won't be around much longer."

"I'm so sorry," Mitchell responded. "I'm so sorry."

"I know, Mitch. We all are. Everybody loves Jack. Now the reason I called you, Jack asked me to call three people whom he insists on talking to before he passes. You're one of them. He'd requested that you come here this Friday. He says it's very important."

"I haven't talked to Coach in so many years, Mrs. Morris. To tell you the truth, it's been so long I'm embarrassed," Mitchell said. "Your husband was always a fine role model for me when I was a youngster, and I've always admired him so much. But I'm puzzled that of all people, I'd be one of three people he wants to see."

"I'm just the messenger, telling you what my husband requested."

"Who are the other two?"

"He also wants Johnny Corleone and Josh Goldman to come in."

"My gosh, I haven't seen Johnny since my graduation. I

read about him in all the business publications. Did he say he'd come?"

"Yes. This Friday, and he's flying in from Boston."

"And Josh Goldman. I bought my first suit that wasn't a hand-me-down at his father's men's shop. Josh was that skinny kid who kicked those three field goals against Jacktown. What's he up to these days?"

"He's a high school teacher in Dayton. I left a message on his machine to call me. Will you come, Mitch, and if so, be here by noon? I'll have lunch waiting."

"Yes, ma'am. I'll be there. You and Coach Morris still live in the same house down from the school?"

"No, we're on North Market Street now."

"No way, Mrs. M. Don't tell me you and Coach live in one of those old Victorian houses we all called Mansion Row? I'm impressed. Sounds like Coach did okay selling real estate."

"He's done well, Johnny. Back in the early '80s, those big houses were selling at all-time lows. They couldn't even give them away. That's when Coach bought the Miller mansion at 800 North Market."

"The Miller house! I know it well. Henry Miller was a big-wig at River Steel, way back when, right? Then the Gibson family bought it, and I used to shovel their snow. And one summer, I helped my father paint it. Sure does bring back old memories. Is that green gazebo still in the backyard? I remember when it was red, but Mrs. Gibson wanted it painted green, so I painted it for her."

"It's still there but now it's red again," Mrs. Morris answered. "Coach and I thought it should be red."

"Yes, I'll come, ma'am."

Her voice cracked again as she said, "Thank you so much, Mitch. My husband and I look forward to seeing you on Friday."

"Same here, Mrs. M."

It was nearly 7:00 when Josh Goldman came home. At 5'8", the trim schoolteacher had a full head of curly dark hair. With his boyish looks and good sense of humor, he was quite popular with his students.

"Sorry I'm late, honey," he said to his wife, Sarah, "but the soccer practice went longer than normal. Where are the kids?"

"I gave them their dinner at six. Maggie's upstairs studying, and Timmy has band practice."

"Yeah, I heard them playing during practice."

"I checked the answering machine this afternoon when I got home from work. There's an interesting message on it for you. It's from Mrs. M. Who's she?"

"Hmm, let me think. Oh yeah, that would be Mrs. Morris. Jack Morris's wife. He's my old high school football coach. I wonder what she wants. I'll call her right now."

"Would you mind talking to her later, honey? Right now we should talk about braces for Maggie." Sarah sighed, taking food out of the refrigerator. "I talked to Dr. Sharp today who said

Maggie needs them now. And braces cost a fortune. I've been thinking about how we can afford it, and I've decided to work the midnight shift at the hospital. The pay is four dollars an hour higher."

"Absolutely not," Josh inserted. "No midnight shift. I'll figure out some other way to supplement my teaching salary."

"Like what?"

"I'll stop coaching soccer and work all summer. I'll moonlight during the school year. I can paint houses during the summer. I'll sell Amway. I can sell real estate."

"I hate to put pressure on you, sweetheart," Sarah said softly. "And you know how frugal I am. If we didn't need the money, I wouldn't even bring the subject up. It's just that the orthodontist is talking about eight thousand dollars."

"Eight thousand dollars!" Josh exclaimed. "Suddenly, I seem to have lost my appetite."

Looking at the worried expression on his wife's face, he said in a calm voice, "Don't worry, honey. We'll find a way to work things out. We always do."

"I know, Josh. But it seems that no matter how hard we work and save, something always comes up and wipes out what little we've got in the bank."

On October 1, 2003, Josh Goldman took a day off from his teaching job to visit his old football coach in Lincoln, Ohio.

Since Dayton was near the Indiana border and Lincoln close to Pennsylvania, it was nearly a four-hour drive across Buckeye Land. Josh filled up the tank of his Honda Accord, calculating that he could make it to Lincoln and halfway back home on a full tank. Normally he didn't like to drive such a long distance alone, but it was a bright, clear autumn day and he looked forward to viewing the gorgeous fall colors. If he had to pick a time of year to drive through his home state, this would be it, when he thought Ohio was most beautiful. He was also anxious to visit Lincoln. He had only been there once since his family moved to the Cleveland area in 1977, and that was for his tenth high school reunion. The reunion was a letdown because the town was even more depressed than Josh had remembered. Most of his classmates had moved out of town, and fewer than half attended the reunion. "It was just too soon," an old classmate commented, "because nobody had done anything significant enough to have earned bragging rights."

During his trip, Josh thought about growing up in Lincoln. What he remembered mostly about his high school days was his father's constant state of depression—by the late '60s Goldman's Clothiers was barely breaking even. As a young man, his dad, Harry Goldman, had migrated to Ohio from the Bronx. He headed west in 1951 to represent the Doubleday Shirt Company. Originally, Harry lived in Cleveland where he met Libby Marks. They were married in 1954, and three years later she bore him a son whom they named Joshua, which they thought was a beautiful biblical name. After the birth, she asked her spouse if it would be possible to consider another line of work, anything that didn't require being on the road. "If a good opportunity comes my way," he assured her, "I'll seriously consider it."

In 1958, Robert Churchill, the owner of Churchill's Haberdashery, Lincoln's leading men's store, announced that he was going to retire. This was the opportunity that Harry Goldman was waiting for. Churchill's was one of Harry's accounts, and he considered it one of the best-managed men's stores in his territory. He was also quite fond of Mr. Churchill, an excellent merchant and a man of high integrity.

When Harry Goldman talked to Churchill about purchasing his business, there were no other interested parties. "Shortly after the steel company shut down," Harry Goldman had told his son, "Mr. Churchill was planning to close the store's doors, so he was thrilled to have a buyer. I had very little money, so I made him an offer with only a small down payment. I signed a ten-year note, and Mr. Churchill accepted my offer in a heartbeat." Shortly after the sale, Mr. Churchill moved to Naples, Florida, and for the next ten years received a monthly check from Harry Goldman.

While Churchill's had a solid reputation, Harry Goldman changed the name to Goldman's. "Churchill was such a WASP name," Josh recalls his father telling him. "I didn't want people to think that a Jew would choose a British-sounding name for fear they would think I was trying to hide my Jewish identity." Reminiscing about his father's reasoning made him chuckle. In Josh's eyes, his father's appearance and thick New York accent were the epitome of the stereotyped Jew. Even if Harry Goldman had changed his surname to Churchill, his Jewishness would remain fully intact.

Josh remembered his father telling him that the store would someday be his. But having witnessed how his father struggled to make ends meet, Josh wanted no part of it. Josh shook his head to shake off the memories and sighed. Funny how thinking about his father's financial struggles reminded him of his own. Coming up with eight thousand for the orthodontist was a frightening thought. It would not only wipe out the family's savings account, it would put them in debt. He momentarily reflected about having Maggie go without braces. For a few brief seconds, a thought raced through his mind of the millions of children all over the world that get by without having their teeth straightened, and they manage to survive. Then he felt ashamed for having such a notion. Maggie will have braces, Josh promised himself.

About halfway to Lincoln and just past Zanesville, Ohio, Josh Goldman's thoughts drifted to Coach Morris and his days as the Lions' kicker. Josh never excelled in sports. He only played football his junior and senior years, and as a kicker, he never identified himself as a jock. With a single exception, his athleticism would have never been remembered by anyone, himself included. That exception was his three field goals in the Lincoln-Jacktown game on November 7, 1975. His performance on that memorable evening was certainly the highlight of his athletic career; nothing in life before or since had come close to matching the high he had felt that night. He had relived his performance a thousand times since, most often when he was down. During low periods, the memory of that night almost always boosted his spirit. It gave him confidence that he was capable of doing whatever he set his mind on doing.

YOU CAN DO WHATEVER YOU SET YOUR MIND ON DOING.

Josh had another recurring thought—one not quite as vivid as visualizing those three amazing field goals sail past the goal post and the corresponding cheers from the crowd. And that was what he experienced the night before. The Pep Talk. At the time, The Pep Talk hardly fazed him. But over the years, he remembered bits and pieces of it, and in time, perhaps even the entire pep talk. *How strange*, he thought, because he could not even recall the man's name who gave it. Nor had he ever discussed it with anyone else. And at the time, because The Pep Talk was Christian-slanted, he felt that it wasn't even meant to be directed at him, the only Jewish player on the 1975 Lincoln squad. Still, in the back of his mind, he subconsciously knew that it somehow had a profound influence on his life. Otherwise, why would he continually dwell on it? Why would he recall parts of it verbatim? Why would he revisit it in his dreams over the course of a quarter of a century?

It took a little more than three hours from the time Johnny Corleone walked out of his elegant townhouse on Nob Hill, Boston's most elite address, got into a limousine, boarded the company Gulf Stream, and arrived at a small airport near Youngstown, Ohio, just thirty-five miles due north of Lincoln, Ohio. Upon landing in Ohio, a shiny Lincoln Continental was waiting for him, a mere twenty yards from where the jet had come to a stop. Corleone folded the map he had studied during his flight to memorize the directions, including a few back roads he recalled from his boyhood that didn't appear on the map.

"I'll call your cell phone when I'm ready to leave Lincoln this afternoon," he told his two pilots. You've got my cell number, right Jack?"

"Yes sir, boss. Enjoy the ride. You sure got a picture-perfect day for it. And drive safely."

Once behind the wheel, Johnny relaxed and enjoyed the ride. As he got nearer to Lincoln, he recognized some old sites he hadn't seen for so many years. He thought about his childhood, and how his father hopped from job to job, always searching for work that would pay high wages like what he earned back in the '50s when he was a foreman in the steel mill. Those were prosperous years before Johnny was born, the ones his dad always referred to as "the good old days."

It wasn't until years after the family had migrated to Toledo that his father again landed a decent factory job at the Jeep plant. All of Johnny's relatives were diligent blue-collar workers who had at one time or another worked in either steel mills or coal mines.

Johnny Corleone was one of the all-time most popular kids at Lincoln High School. He was good looking, a scholar-athlete, and just a really nice kid. He was a better scholar than an athlete—remember now, the Lions had their worst-ever record during his helm as the Lions' quarterback. However, Lincoln was a workingman's town, so with the exception of a few members of the teaching staff, nobody really paid much attention to his academic achievements. Above all else, Johnny was an excellent leader. As an adult, he sometimes attributed his leadership skills to the time he spent quarterbacking a horrendous football team. "Speaking about adversity, I learned considerably more about leadership by playing on a losing team," he was fond of saying at management seminars when making reference to his high school football days.

Johnny also frequently quoted Ernest Hemingway's *Farewell to Arms* when he spoke about adversity. "The world breaks everyone, and afterward many are stronger at the broken places," he often told young bank employees.

When his motorcycle accident ended his football career, he took it in stride. Johnny knew he had no future in football after high school. He considered the team's poor record as somewhat of an embarrassment, but nothing he was ashamed about. After all, football was only a game. He enjoyed playing it, and in particular he loved the camaraderie. Win or lose, he was a team player, a quality that served him well throughout his career.

There was in reality only a single time when he excelled on the football field. And that was the night he completed twenty out of twenty-eight passes against Jacktown. The Game. He never forgot the excitement of that game. How well he remembered the adrenalin that shot through his entire body! The excitement of the crowd. The satisfaction of knowing he was in control of his destiny. The bonding he felt that night with his teammates. The trust he had in them, knowing that each play relied on the execution of every member of the squad doing his job. And of course the trust they had in him. It was a team effort. Oftentimes afterward, Johnny would re-create the game in his mind. He especially enjoyed the exhilaration he felt knowing that when he flung the football, it was destined to arrive at its exact destination. That night, it was as if he was releasing guided missiles instead of throwing passes. He *knew* every pass he threw would find its intended receiver. It didn't matter that the destination was a moving target. All the pieces had fallen together during that magical game, and it was a thrill that Johnny never forgot. Nor did he ever want to forget. This is why he continually played mental reruns of The Game. And each time he did, he'd get a high.

It was strange how that one game had erased all of the booing that Johnny and his teammates endured during their

eak. All of those losses. Game after game after
hile, it seemed as if the team would never win
hen it came time to play his last football game
ᵥₑᵣ ₐg acktown, nobody in town gave them a chance
over the mighty Giants. Yes, most of his football memories
were about disappointments. But the only one that really mattered to Johnny Corleone was the way their team performed
in The Game. Oh, and something else crossed his mind as he
cruised down the back roads: The Pep Talk that was given to
the team the night before. Johnny had never forgotten it. It
was given by a Mr. What's-his-name?

For years Johnny had racked his brain trying to remember
who it was that gave that pep talk. It was funny that he couldn't
remember the stranger's name, but he was positive that the
man wore a fedora with a red feather in the hatband. Johnny
couldn't visualize what he looked like at all, except for the hat
he wore. Even odder was the fact that he remembered the
man's message in amazing detail. He remembered hearing
Joshua 1:9, a scripture that he since frequently quoted: "Be
strong and courageous; do not be frightened or dismayed for
the LORD your God is with you wherever you go." Johnny had
repeated these words to himself as well as to others many
times. Most importantly, this scripture had aided him through
difficult times during the course of his life.

Johnny also prayed a great deal, and he wasn't shy about
telling people that he prayed—he even talked about prayer at
business meetings. It didn't matter who was present, he fre-

quently quoted Mark 11:24: "Whatever you ask for in prayer, believe that you have received it, and it will be yours." Afterward, he was prone to add, "I know because I have prayed and I have received."

Mark Mitchell drove a big black Mercedes to Lincoln. He left just before 9:00 a.m., even though it was only a two-and-a-half-hour ride from Columbus. It had been quite some time since his last visit to Lincoln, and once on the road, like Josh and Johnny, he also began to think about what it was like growing up in a small town three decades ago; it seemed light years away from his life now. After he graduated from high school, he was a page in the Ohio Senate during college, thanks to Irwin Benson, a state senator from Lincoln who pulled some strings to land him the job. In the summers, he had painted houses with his father.

"I want you to have a good education and make something of yourself," Mark remembered his father repeatedly telling him as they worked. "I don't want you to spend your life painting houses like your old man. You're better than that."

Thinking about his father made Mark's eyes water, and tears started running down his cheeks. It had been years since he had cried, and he found it somewhat embarrassing. No, not embarrassing, more like humbling. He wished that his father was alive to enjoy his success at the bank. He would have been so proud. Mark had always thrived on making his father feel proud.

Mark remembered how proud his father was when he became the starting linebacker for the Lincoln Lions. He also recalled his father telling him not to be discouraged during the team's long, long losing streak. As he drove to Lincoln, Mark laughed out loud when he thought about his father's corny saying: "It's not the dog in the fight that counts. It's the fight in the dog that counts." And as corny as he found the quote, he often used the same line when addressing bank employees.

About halfway to Lincoln, his thoughts drifted to The Pep Talk. Like Johnny and Josh, he had also thought about it over the years, and like they, he remembered bits and pieces of parts; some he summoned up verbatim. He began thinking about The Game, and in particular, how he played at a level that he never dreamed he was capable of playing. *I was everywhere on the field that night*, Mark remembered. *I played my heart out because I didn't want to let my teammates down. I only weighed 165 pounds, and I was making hits against Jacktown players twice my size. I was fearless.*

Although he never again had a repeat performance on the football field that came anywhere close to how he played in the big game, the knowledge that he had excelled had given him confidence to strive for more ambitious goals later in his life. He believed that anything is possible, no matter how great the odds are. "I can accomplish anything that I set my mind on. 'Blessed are those who have not seen and yet have come to believe,'" he said out loud. "John 20:29." Throughout his life, those words had served him well.

THE REUNION

Having the shortest distance to travel, Mark was the first to arrive in Lincoln. Once inside the city limits, he passed by the big steel mill on the south side of town. It was still there, a shadow of its former self. Fifty years later, the mill remained unoccupied—all three million square feet of it, an eyesore of nearly seventy acres. The humongous black structure was rusted; every window was shattered and boarded up. Its huge smoke stacks seemed to sag and lean over. Weeds and trees had grown through its asphalted parking lot. A chain fence topped with barbed wire surrounded it with big, bold signs warning trespassers to stay away or be prosecuted.

Once past the industrial section of town, Mark drove down Main Street through the downtown area for old times' sake. Only having to stop for one of the three traffic lights in the six-block business section, he covered Lincoln's main thorough-fare in less than forty seconds. Downtown Lincoln looked similar to how he remembered it. The three drug stores had been replaced by a Wendy's, a Subway, and a used bookstore, though. And there was no more Goldman's. It was a boarded-up storefront. One of his own State National Bank branches occupied the corner lot that had once been a Gulf Oil Station. Another sight that would have pleased his dad.

Mark took a left turn on North Market, and a few blocks away from the commercial area stood those magnificent Victorian homes that he admired as a boy. He was surprised that these stately residences were as big as he remembered. *These noble homes have withstood the test of time*, he thought to himself.

Spotting the 800 North Market Street address, Mark immediately recognized the old Miller Mansion, one of the biggest houses in the county. The house was built in 1912. Mark parked near the curb and walked up the driveway.

Margaret Morris greeted him at the door. "You're . . ."

"Mitch," he answered. "Mrs. M., you haven't changed at all."

"You certainly have," she replied. "Of course, you were just a boy when I last saw you. Now look at you. You look taller than I remembered, and you've added a few pounds."

"I was only seventeen when I graduated Lincoln, and you're right ma'am. I grew another two inches in my freshman year at OSU, and today I'm twenty pounds heavier. Had I had another year in high school, I might have been a better football player for Coach."

"Coach and I have followed your career," she said. "Who

would have ever imagined you'd be a big-shot banker?" Changing the subject she said, "My husband is in the library. This is the first time this week he's been out of the bedroom. Thank the Lord, Coach is having a good day. I'm sure knowing the three of you would be here today has boosted his spirits. Come on, let's go see him."

"One of your boys is here," she announced, opening the door to the library. Jack Morris was in his pajamas, wearing a navy bathrobe, and sitting in a leather chair behind his desk.

Mark didn't show it when he entered the room, but had the truth been known, he would not have recognized his former football coach. Morris was a shell of the sturdy man Mark remembered. He looked considerably older than his seventy-plus years.

"Great to see you, Coach. You haven't changed one iota over the years."

"Well, you sure have, Mitch," Morris said in a weak voice. "For the better, I might add."

"Quite a pad you've got here, Coach. I take it the real estate business agrees with you."

"I've done okay," Morris replied. "I applied the same stuff I taught you guys in football—it works in business too."

"Like what?"

"For starters, discipline," Coach said. "You've got to be a self-starter to sell real estate 'cause you're your own boss. You come and go as you please. No fixed hours. Then too, you've got to be prepared. You must do your homework before you show a property—this is an area where most real estate people are weak. By doing my homework, I always felt as if I had an edge on the competition. And like most businesses, it's about building relationships with people. Oops, sorry, Mitch, but you got me started."

"No, no. I hear you, Coach. Sounds like the same principles that work in the banking business.

"Driving up Market Street, I noticed how well maintained these Victorian homes are," Mark said. "With the depressed economic conditions in Lincoln, I thought they'd be rooming houses and converted into low-end apartments."

"It was a matter of civic pride," Morris said. "As a realtor, I headed a campaign to save these houses. Made sure the zoning laws prevented them from deteriorating."

Twenty minutes later Josh Goldman walked in the door, and just before noon, Johnny Corleone arrived. "All present and accounted for," Morris said. After the four men had become reacquainted, at 12:30 Margaret Morris brought in a tray with soup and sandwiches. She left the room and returned with a tray of potato chips, homemade cookies, and soft drinks.

"So Coach, you didn't do too bad for yourself," Johnny said, looking at the coach's spacious study.

"Those real estate commissions sure beat a teacher's salary, didn't they, Coach?" Josh said.

"True," Morris commented, "but they never came close to giving me the job satisfaction that came from working with young people.

"When you get to the stage of life where I am," he added, "the amount of money you've accumulated is not what matters. It's what you've done for others."

> IT'S NOT ABOUT THE AMOUNT OF MONEY YOU'VE
> ACCUMULATED, BUT WHAT YOU'VE DONE FOR OTHERS.

"I'm with you on that," Johnny said, and Mark nodded.

"It's easy for you two to say," Josh teased. "You guys are zillionaires. What's Alpha's stock trading at these days, Johnny? I read that every time it goes up a point, you make another few million. And Mark, how much are your State National stock options worth these days?"

"All three of you have been very successful in your line of work," Jack Morris butted in. "I'm equally proud of each of you. Say, did you two know that last April, Josh was named Ohio Teacher of the Year?"

"No, but that's quite an honor," Johnny said.

"Congratulations," Mark said, patting his friend on the back.

"Guys, there is something I want to talk to the three of you about," Morris broke in. "It's something that's been on my mind for a very long time. I know Mrs. M. has told you about my tumor and that I'm not long for this world. Well, the truth is, guys, I invited the three of you here because I need some answers that you just might have for me before I check out of here . . ." The old man's voice cracked, and he stopped in the middle of his sentence.

"I was wondering why you asked us," Mark said, breaking the pause in the conversation. "If it were just me and Johnny, I'd think it was because of our good looks. But then Josh is here so that's ruled out."

Nobody laughed. It was not a time for levity.

"You've got us intrigued, Coach. What's up?" Johnny asked.

"And why us?" Josh added.

"Now where do I start?" Jack Morris said with a slight hesitation. "Let's go back to what has been referred to as 'The Game.' The night we beat Jacktown."

"When people hear I'm from Lincoln," Josh interjected, "the first thing they ask is, 'Were you at The Game?' I've had strangers tell me that the Lincoln kicker had three field goals, all from more than 50 yards out."

"Just last week, there was an article in the *Columbus Dispatch* that mentioned The Game," Mark grinned. "For years, they've been comparing upsets of major Ohio teams to the Lincoln-Jacktown game."

"I didn't suppose any of you would forget that game," Coach Morris said, "but what I really need to know is this: Do any of you remember anything about The Pep Talk the night before the game?"

At the following silence, a look of disappointment appeared on Coach's face. "I thought for sure that one of you . . ." Morris started to say. "Doesn't it ring a bell? Do any of you . . ."

"Yes, I remember it very well," Corleone volunteered. Then Mark and Goldman nodded their heads confirming that they also remembered it.

"Does anyone care to elaborate?" Morris asked.

At first nobody volunteered. Following a few moments of silence, Mark quietly said, "Yes. I've thought about it quite a bit over the years. Indeed, I confess that I think about it quite often. As a matter of fact, just today, on my drive here from Columbus, I was thinking about it."

"Oddly enough, me too," Josh said sheepishly.

"Do you mean you think about it like Mitch?" Johnny asked, "or you just happened to think about it on your way here today?"

"Both. It's as if I've never gotten that pep talk out of my mind. And like Mitch, coming here today, I visualized myself sitting there in the locker room that night, listening to that stranger with the fancy hat. All the while, I was taking in everything that the man said."

Getting up out of his chair, Corleone said, "This conversation is giving me goose bumps. Let me tell you something that I've never told anyone before, not even my wife. I can remember so much of what that man told us that night that it's downright eerie. The fact is, I can't begin to tell you what an influence it's had on my life. You've all heard about something happening to a person that he refers to as a defining moment in his life. I believe that's how The Pep Talk affected me."

"I can't begin to express how much hearing you say that means to me," Morris interrupted, his face lighting up.

"How's that, Coach?" Corleone asked.

"It's had a lasting effect on me too. However, I've talked to many of the other players over the last few years, and nobody, and I mean nobody, had even a vague recollection about The Pep Talk. Some said they thought I might have said something to the team that got them fired up, but that's it. Nobody remembers Mr. Christopher."

"Christopher, that's his name!" Corleone exclaimed. "I couldn't remember his name to save my life."

"Nor could I," said Goldman, "but I have a vague recollection about what he looked like. Just the same, I wouldn't want the responsibility of having to identify him in a police lineup. Unless of course he was the only one wearing a tweed hat with a red feather in the hatband."

"Right," Johnny chimed in, "the man wore a fedora, and yes, it had a red feather. Reminded me of Bear Bryant. I'm referring to the hat, not Mr. Christopher. Strange, how you remember a small detail like that, isn't it?"

"How 'bout you, Mitch?" Coach asked.

"I'm not sure I ever did catch his name, but I certainly remember him, and yes, the hat," Mark said. "Tell us about him, Coach. Who was he?"

"Not much to tell," Morris answered. "Early that morning,

I met the man at Abe's Lincoln Diner. He introduced himself and joined me for a cup of coffee. Said he was a stranger in town. I reckoned he was a salesman traveling through. We got to shooting the breeze and before I knew it, he said he'd like to give a pep talk to the team and I okayed it. Now for the life of me, I couldn't tell you why I consented to let a stranger give a talk to the team, particularly a man who was only thirty-something. Just the same, there was something I liked about him. He was so sincere and he had a nice, pleasant way."

"He was only thirty?" Mark said. "He seemed older. Of course when you're seventeen, anyone over twenty-five is ancient."

"What about after The Pep Talk? Josh asked. "What did you talk about with him?"

"Before I could thank him, he was out of there. Never saw him again. The truth is, at the time I wasn't even sure that what he said meant anything to any of you guys."

"Yeah, I remember there was a lull in the room after he finished," Mark said. "No stir whatsoever. Just silence."

"It was as if the team couldn't make heads or tails of his message," Josh said.

"It wasn't the kind of pep talk you expect to hear in locker rooms," Johnny said. "It was more like something you'd hear in church. But that's not quite it either. I remember how he quoted the *Bhagavad Gita*. I don't think any of us had ever heard of it back then. I didn't know what the *Bhagavad Gita* was until my senior year in college when a professor talked about dharma during a lecture on Eastern philosophy. Like I say, a lot of what this Mr. Christopher said probably went over our heads, hence the silent reaction when he finished."

"A few weeks later, I was still thinking about his pep talk," Morris interjected. "I wanted to talk to him about it. I wanted to thank him, so I started to do some inquiring. Now, remember there was no Internet—I couldn't go online to do a search on him. Mr. Christopher said he was originally from Bethlehem, a steel town in Eastern Pennsylvania with a big reputation in sports for its great athletes. I called all of the high school football coaches in the Lehigh Valley, but nobody ever heard hide nor hair of him. I even mentioned the fedora. I remembered that Mr. Christopher said he grew up in the area and had moved to Philadelphia. I never did know his first name, and Philadelphia is too big a city to find a 'Mr. Christopher,' so I gave up trying to find him. However, every now and then I'd meet someone from Philly, and when I did, I'd describe our Mr. Christopher and what I knew about him. But nobody ever knew anyone that fit his description."

"Anyone in Lincoln know anything about him? You said he was driving through. If he was in the diner at 6:00 a.m., he must have stayed somewhere nearby," Mark questioned.

"Good thinking, Mitch," Morris said, "and I did call the River Hotel and all the motels in the area. Again, I struck out."

"What about the waitress? Did she know anything about him?"

"That was Beatrice. She was the only one in the diner during the time Mr. Christopher and I were there," Morris said. "She said, 'I only vaguely remember you talking to someone, but what do I know? So many customers passing through every week. They come and they go.' She was clueless. She couldn't even remember his fedora.

"Not being able to find him really got to me," Morris continued. "Every now and then, I'd be walking down the street, or at a public place like an Ohio State football game, and I'd spot a guy wearing a fedora. So I was always being reminded of him. More than once, I'd see a man wearing a fedora walking with his back toward me, and I'd run to get ahead of him to see if he was Mr. Christopher. Like I said, it really got to me."

"Why was it so important for you to talk to him, Coach?" Johnny asked.

"I can't honestly answer that question, Johnny," Morris sighed and shrugged his shoulders. "I suppose there was just something about him that got to me. You know, how we played the game of our lives against Jacktown. Quite frankly, there was no way I thought we could beat them. They were far superior athletes in every position. And well coached. Jacktown's head coach, Rich Hart, later coached at Texas Southern.

"After I retired as head coach and started selling real estate full-time, I reflected about the Jacktown game. I kept asking myself what we did to win that game. It was as if a guardian angel was watching over us. We could do no wrong . . . Josh making those three field goals. With all due respect Josh, you never hit one from thirty-four yards out before that game.

Johnny competed twenty for twenty-nine and ran the ball magnificently. And you, Mitch, twenty-four tackles. Come on guys. You were all playing so far over your heads—and against Jacktown.

"Well, I started thinking about it, and the only thing I could figure that was different from our other games was The Pep Talk. But I couldn't make any sense out of it. One thing the four of us do know—it was no ordinary pep talk. Look at how it's stuck with each of you all of your lives. Can you remember anything about any other pep talk you ever heard? You've heard me give them at practices, before games, at halftimes."

"Not really, Coach," Josh said. "I can't honestly remember one of yours other than the fact that you gave them. It was just so long ago, Coach. But what I can't get over is how well I do remember Mr. Christopher's pep talk."

"Okay, so we all remember it," Johnny said. "There are lots of things we hear when we're kids that stay with us. Particularly when we're young and impressionable."

BELIEVE IN YOURSELF.

"Actually," Mark inserted, "I do remember one pep talk you gave us that was by far your best. The one I'm referring to was at halftime during The Game."

"Oh yes, and it was a good one," Johnny said. "I remember it too. You told us that the Jacktown Giants were not giants after all, and you reminded us that we had hung in there with them for the first half, and that if we could do it for the first two quarters, we could do it for the next two. You made us believe in ourselves."

"Yes, I remember that one too," Josh added. "You told us not to focus on the scoreboard and to execute our individual assignment—one play at a time. And trust. You emphasized trust. Trust each of our teammates to do his assignment. Yes, and you told the linemen to 'master the box,' and you said we should just keep planting grass. You said a lot of the things that Mr. Christopher had told us during The Pep Talk."

"You also quoted Mark 11:24: 'Whatever you ask for in prayer, believe that you have received it, and it will be yours,'" Johnny said. And you asked us to say a prayer before the start of the second half. You're right, Mitch, that was Coach's best ever pep talk. You really had us fired up for the second half."

"Thanks for the vote of confidence," Morris said. "Now I've got something to show you, and this is going to blow your minds. I've put together a scrapbook. Once you see it, I think you'll understand why I wanted you here today."

THE SCRAPBOOK

J ack Morris slowly walked across the spacious room to
retrieve a large scrapbook from the bookshelf on the far side
of the study.

"You're holding that like it's the Holy Grail," Johnny
remarked.

"Well put," Morris answered, placing the large scrapbook
on the desk. "It may very well be the Holy Grail.'"

"A few weeks ago, Margaret brought down from the attic all
these old boxes containing photos and news clippings,"
Morris said, pointing to the other side of the room. "She
thought it would be good therapy for me to go through them.
I went along with her, mostly to appease her. But she was
right. The old memories did turn out to be therapeutic. They
took my mind off my illness. I don't know why but I started to
categorize everything chronologically," Morris continued,
flipping through pages of the scrapbook. "This is when I

came across these old news clippings about the Jacktown game.

"Forget about all the other stuff," Morris continued, pointing to the opened scrapbook. "I want you to look at the articles on these pages. Starting here with the part about the Jacktown game. Here's where it starts to get really interesting."

His three guests stood behind him, looking over his shoulder. "Pay close attention to these articles in particular," Morris instructed.

The headlines read:

MARK MITCHELL BREAKS UP 11 PASSES, HAS 24 TACKLES

JOHNNY CORLEONE COMPLETES 20 OUT OF 29

KICKER JOSH GOLDMAN, NUMBER 1, OUTSCORES JACKTOWN WITH 9

"I remember those articles," Josh said.

Morris pulled out Xeroxed copies of the three articles and with a yellow highlight pen, he said, "Now watch carefully."

In the first article, he highlighted MARK, 11, and 24.

In the second article he highlighted JOHN, 20, and 29.

In the third article he highlighted JOSH, 1, and 9. After the word JOSH, he added the letters UA.

"Have any of you figured out what I've done?" he asked.

Nobody said a word. "Look what we got here," he said as he wrote on a legal pad in big, bold letters:

MARK 11:24.

JOHN 20:29

JOSHUA 1:9

"Now do you get it?"

"Bible verses," Josh said. "But what's it mean?"

"Before I explain, let me quote scripture to you," Coach Morris continued. "Mark 11:24 reads, 'Whatever you ask for in prayer, believe that you have received it, and it will be yours.'"

"I can take it from here, Coach," Johnny said. "John 20:29 reads, 'Blessed are those who have not seen and yet have come to believe.'" Then he added, "'Be strong and courageous; do not be frightened or dismayed, for the LORD your God is with you wherever you go.' That's Joshua 1:9."

"You know your Bible well," Mitch said. "I'm impressed."

"I'm not as good as you think," Johnny answered. "I happen to know those three passages because they were the scriptures that Mr. Christopher quoted in his pep talk. Somehow, deep in here somewhere," he continued, placing his index finger to his head, "Mr. Christopher's words got to me. I can't quote much from the Bible, but I do know those scriptures."

"Were there any other scriptures spoken by Mr. Christopher?" Mark asked.

"Yes, one more," Morris answered.

"That's right," Mitch volunteered. "He quoted one of my favorite verses, which is John 15:12. It's where Christ says,

'This is my commandment, that you love one another as I have loved you.' Any articles make reference to this one?"

"No, Mitch. None that I've come across," Morris replied.

"So what's this all mean?" Josh asked.

"That's why I asked you all to come," Morris said. "It's been on my mind ever since I started putting this scrapbook together, but I'm not sure what to make of it.

"One thing I do know," he added. "I sure don't want to be lying on my deathbed never knowing the answer. And the way things stand now, that's a definite possibility."

Nobody said a word. Then Johnny spoke, carefully choosing his words. "I'm thinking out loud on this one, guys. Now bear with me. Here are the facts as we know them. Number one: This Mr. Christopher came out of nowhere. He was an absolute stranger who gave a pep talk that all of us heard many years ago, and yet the four of us here in this room clearly remember parts of it as if it were yesterday."

"Two: According to Coach, none of the other guys who were there seem to recall The Pep Talk," Mark added.

"And three: We three players are the only ones about whom there is corresponding scripture," Josh said, "and most baffling is the fact that this Mr. Christopher used these references before the game."

"Exactly," Morris interrupted, "scripture that matched your names with your performances in the game, and in your case Josh, your jersey number and your nine points. Think about it, boys. What can it possibly mean?"

The room was once again very quiet. Finally, Josh broke the silence. "If I may, I ask for your permission to play the role of devil's advocate."

"By all means," Mark said.

"I recently had a discussion with my eleventh-grade history students," Josh said, "that I think is applicable to what has happened here. I am sure you've heard about the famous Abraham Lincoln and John Kennedy coincidences, but please bear with me and allow me to finish so I can make my point.

"Lincoln was elected to Congress in 1846. Kennedy was elected to Congress in 1946. Lincoln was elected president in 1860, Kennedy in 1960. The names Lincoln and Kennedy each contain seven letters. Both wives lost their children while living in the White House. Both presidents were shot on a Friday, and both in the head."

"I'm familiar with what you're saying," Mark said. "Both were assassinated by Southerners, and both were succeeded by Southerners. Both successors were named Johnson."

"Very good, Mitch," Johnny said. "That would be Andrew Johnson, who succeeded Lincoln and was born in 1808, and Lyndon Johnson, who succeeded Kennedy and was born in 1908. I also remember reading that John Wilkes Booth, who assassinated Lincoln, was born in 1839 and Lee Harvey Oswald who shot Kennedy was born in 1939."

"You got it," Josh interrupted, "and both assassins were known by their three names, and each had a name with fifteen letters. Booth ran from a theater and was caught in a warehouse while Oswald ran from a warehouse and was caught in a theater. Lincoln was shot at the Ford Theater, and Kennedy was shot in a Lincoln car, a Ford product. And Booth and Oswald were assassinated before their trials. Did you know that Lincoln's secretary was Ms. Kennedy and Kennedy's secretary was Ms. Lincoln?

"The message I gave to my class was that these were coincidences and nothing more. For instance, I pointed out to my students that the list only includes facts and figures that are coincidences but the list excludes what are not. Lincoln was born in 1809 and Kennedy in 1917—if a list is composed of the coincidences it should also include non-related facts and figures. For example, Lincoln had four sons while Kennedy had a son and a daughter. Lincoln's son was not killed in a plane crash, nor did Lincoln have a brother who was attorney general and was assassinated. I also told my students that if you're going to talk about the number of letters in their names, why not also mention that Booth's full name has three letter *o*'s as compared to one letter *o* for Oswald. Do you see where I'm going with this?"

"I suppose I'm just a dying old man who's grasping for straws," Morris sighed. "Thanks, Josh. What you just said makes a lot of sense."

Seeing the old man's disappointment, Josh said, "Not so fast, Coach. Like I said, I was playing the devil's advocate, but that doesn't mean I know what to make of this. What incredible odds that Mr. Christopher could have made reference to specific scriptures in The Pep Talk that would correspond with the game stats and then appear in those news clippings. Look at those three headlines in the newspaper—and look at what you've highlighted with our names matching our numbers and our performances. Johnny completing twenty out of twenty-nine passes. Mark, a.k.a. Mitch, breaking up eleven passes and having twenty-four tackles. And then there I am—Number 1 with those three field goals for nine points."

"Also consider the profound impact that The Pep Talk had on each of our lives," Mark interjected. "How do you account for that? I concur with Josh's comparisons between Lincoln and Kennedy. There are lots of coincidences. Just pure coincidences. But I refuse to accept The Pep Talk and the consequences that occurred in The Game and the effects it had on our lives as coincidental."

"Then what do you make of it?" Coach asked.

"It was God-inspired," Mark said. "I believe it was God-inspired."

"Like a miracle from biblical times?" Josh questioned.

"Why not?" Johnny asked.

"You know, billions of people in this world pray to God every day," Mark said. "We talk to Him in our prayers. We audibly give thanks to Him in church and at mealtimes. But if someone tells you that God talked to him, people say he's crazy. Well, I do believe God talks to us. We may not hear His voice, but He does communicate to us in other ways. He does it when He answers our prayers. He does it when He blesses us. And I'm sure He does it when He furnishes us with good thoughts, gives us courage, and fills our hearts with love. Gentlemen, allow me to quote John 20:29 once again: 'Blessed are those who have not seen and yet have come to believe.' Is it necessary for God to appear in this room in order for us to come up with a definite and logical explanation about what happened? Is that what we must have in order to believe in God's work?'"

"Amen, Brother Mitch," Josh said. "Well put."

"Boys, I am so grateful to you for visiting me today," Coach said. "I can't begin to tell you how much this has meant to me."

"Speaking for Josh and Mitch," Johnny said, "it's meant so much to all of us, and we thank you."

"Seconded," Josh and Mark said in unison.

"I'm exhausted, boys, and need to take my nap," Morris said. "If one of you will help me to that sofa over there."

"Can you believe, it's nearly four o'clock," Josh said, glancing at his watch for the first time since they'd arrived.

The three men said their good-byes to their old coach and promised to keep in touch with him. Margaret Morris came in with a blanket and covered her husband who was now resting comfortably on the sofa. She gently kissed him on the forehead and walked her visitors to the door. After exchanging hugs, her parting words were, "It's meant so much to Coach for you to be here today."

Walking to their cars, Mark said, "I think the three of us should have a little chat before we go our separate ways. What do you say we stop at Abe's Lincoln Diner for coffee?

Do you have an extra half hour to spare, Johnny, before you catch your plane?"

"My plane isn't going anywhere without me," Johnny said. "How about you, Josh?"

"Let's do it."

COFFEE AT THE DINER

At 4:00 in the afternoon, a slow time of the day, the diner was empty. The diner's walls were covered with sports paraphernalia, most of which was devoted to the Lincoln Lions' football conquests of yesteryear.

"I think we might as well sit at this table," Johnny suggested, pointing to a seat beneath a framed article about The Game.

Seated at a booth in the back of the diner, Johnny said, "Take a look at this place. It's as if we're in a time warp—everything's exactly like I remember it."

"I expect old Abe to come marching out from the back any second now," Mark said, and turning to the waitress asked, "We'd like some coffee, ma'am, and hey, does Abe Horowitz still own this place?"

"Who?" questioned the young girl, oblivious to the fact that Abe Horowitz was the founder and former owner of where she worked.

"Never mind, you just answered my question," Mark said.

When the waitress returned to the table with three coffees, Johnny pointed to the framed article on the wall and said, "I bet the people in this town still talk about that one. Is that right, ma'am?"

"It was played long before I was born," she smiled, "but yes, they still talk about it. My dad was at the game, and every football season, I hear him talking about it with my uncles."

After the waitress walked away, Mark said, "Now that we're no longer in the presence of Coach Morris, we can talk more freely. I'm sure you both caught the look of disappointment on his face when Josh started in about the Lincoln/Kennedy coincidences. I don't know what exactly to make out of the whole rigmarole, but one thing I do know is that we must be careful not to burst his bubble. If he has it in his mind that this is God-inspired, so be it. Let's let him keep on thinking it. There's nothing wrong about a man on his deathbed being consumed with such thoughts."

"And are you so sure that he's wrong?" Johnny asked.

"Not at all," Mark answered. "But then there is always the possibility that just maybe he is. And at the risk of sounding like a Doubting Thomas, I'm of the opinion that the three of us should do everything we possibly can to prove or disprove what Coach thinks. Now don't get me wrong, guys. It's not as if I lack conviction in the Scriptures. Remember, the Good Book tells us that faith is believing in the unseen, and for the record, I buy into that hook, line, and sinker. Having said that,

I think we should exercise due diligence so we can figure out just what this is all about."

"I apologize for bringing up that Lincoln/Kennedy analogy," Josh offered. "It's just my nature to play the devil's advocate, and sometimes I do it to my own detriment because I cast a shadow of a doubt on what I actually believe. It must be the teacher in me. I find myself challenging the facts, never wanting to accept anything as it appears on the surface."

"That's not all so bad," Mark said. "We do the same thing in business."

"Am I reading you two right?" Johnny said thoughtfully. "I surmise from what I am hearing that you are both saying that maybe Coach is on to something. But before we write this whole thing off, we should collectively work together to get some concrete answers. Am I on the same page with you guys?"

"I won't speak for Josh, but I believe this merits delving into."

"I agree," Josh said. "Like we discussed at Coach's, that pep talk has been programmed in my mind, and apparently in yours too. This by itself warrants further exploration."

"That," pondered Johnny, "plus the scriptures thing. That's what truly baffles me. Sure, there may be some logical explanation, but if there is one, it sure has me stumped."

"We had a speaker at a retreat last year who told a wonderful story," Mark said. Now it's fairly long, but it's worth repeating because its message is so appropriate. It goes like this: There are four people on a train en route from Paris to Barcelona—a beautiful young girl traveling with her elderly grandmother, and a stately general traveling with his aide, a young, handsome second lieutenant. The foursome is sitting in silence as the train enters a tunnel in the Pyrenees, the mountain range on the border between France and Spain.

"It is pitch-dark in the tunnel. Suddenly there's the sound of a loud kiss, followed by a second sound, that of a loud, hard smack. Upon exiting the tunnel, the four people remain silent, with no one acknowledging the incident.

"The young girl thinks to herself, *Boy, that was a swell kiss that good-looking lieutenant gave me, and I really enjoyed it. What a shame my grandmother slapped him, because he must have thought it was I who slapped him. That's too bad, because when we get to the next tunnel, he won't kiss me again.*

"The grandmother thinks, *That fresh young man kissed my granddaughter. But fortunately I brought her up to be a lady, so she slapped him real good. I'm glad because now he'll stay away from her when we get to the next tunnel.*

"The general thinks to himself, *I can't believe what just happened. I personally handpicked him to be my aide, and I thought he was a real gentleman. But in the dark, he took advantage of that young girl and kissed her. But she must have thought it was I who kissed her, since I was the one she slapped.*

"Meanwhile, I young lieutenant is thinking, *Boy, that was wonderful. How often do you get to kiss a beautiful girl and slug your boss at the same time?*

"The story shows that while four people can have the same set of facts, they can arrive at four different conclusions. My point is, there is a possibility we can all disagree on what happened after we have all of the facts."

"Good analogy," Johnny said, "and sure, it is a definite possibility that we may never reach a conclusion that we can agree on. It wouldn't surprise me in the least if that's what happens."

"You guys are big-shot executives," Josh said. "If this were a business situation, how would you approach it? And please, no committees."

"The first thing we'd do at the bank," said Mark, "would involve conducting a thorough investigation on Mr. Christopher. We'd want to find out everything we could on him. And believe me, by the end of the day, we'd know all about him, including what he ate for breakfast and his preferred brand of toothpaste."

"Obviously you're talking about something more extensive than running a credit report," Josh joked.

"Exactly. What I have in mind will be more on the order of what we'd do if we were hiring a key executive," Mark replied. "The bank has some good internal people, plus we contract outside sources that are specialists at this sort of thing. If there is a Mr. Christopher or there has ever been a Mr. Christopher, by the time they're through, we'll know all about him. Trust me—everything."

"Even going back to the 1970s, and with the little information Coach told us?" Josh questioned.

"I've seen investigations go back a lot further than twenty-eight years," Mark stressed with conviction. "Besides, we have plenty of information to conduct a thorough search. We know the man's last name and that he lived in Bethlehem, and later in Philadelphia."

"His work also required him to come to Ohio," Johnny added.

"Yes, and I remember when he was being introduced to us at The Pep Talk," Josh recalled. "Didn't Coach say that Mr. Christopher spoke to other football teams, including the Cleveland Browns and Philadelphia Eagles?"

"Right, he did say that," Mark said in surprise. "It sounds like we got enough leads to track down Mr. Christopher."

"How can you be so sure?" Josh quizzed Mark. "We're talking about more than a quarter of a century ago."

"I don't know how these guys do it, but our people are professionals at this," Mark said. "Josh, you're the historian. Look how they research events that occurred going back centuries."

"Okay, we do a search for Mr. Christopher," Johnny said. "And with the use of the Internet, I agree, it is doable. Any other ideas?"

"We have some very smart numbers people at the bank," Mark said. "Some of our guys are brilliant mathematicians. I feel confident that when we give them those numbers with our names, they'll have some interesting interpretations. For instance, what are the odds of Mr. Christopher quoting Mark 11:24 in a pep talk before the game, and a player named Mark blocking eleven passes and making twenty-four tackles? Now, those odds must be astronomically high. And then when it happens two more times with John 20:29 and Joshua 1:9. I'm telling you, the odds must be off the charts."

"While your guys at the bank are doing that," Johnny inserted, "I'll have some of our technology experts search the Internet for articles on other sports events that match scripture. Certainly, there will be some match-ups, and if so, they'll follow up to see if any are relevant."

"Have them make inquiries on whether Mr. Christopher or some other character appears out of the woodwork who delivered a pep talk," Mark suggested. "I recommend that they run a search going back to the late 1960s through the present. As far fetched as it sounds, that may be how we track our Mr. Christopher down. We should not assume that we were the only team that he ever gave a pep talk to that had these results."

"Excellent point," Johnny said. "I think we're on the right track. What else can we do?"

"I've got one," Josh answered. "I recommend that we each record everything we remember about Mr. Christopher's pep talk. We'll do it independently, and afterward, let's see how much our recollections match."

"Great idea," Johnny said. "Let's do it over the weekend so we don't lose any momentum. I have a tape recorder on the plane. I'll start my recording during my flight to Cape Cod. My secretary will transcribe it on Monday."

"You and Mitch can e-mail your recollections to me. I'll review them after all my thoughts are down on paper. Then I'll compare them, and afterward I'll make an attempt to reconstruct The Pep Talk. Wouldn't it be something if between the three of us, we can replicate most of it? Wouldn't you like to hear it again?"

"This is like how the police have an artist draw a composite of an individual seen at a crime scene by several witnesses," added Johnny, his face lighting up.

"I spotted a Radio Shack on Main Street," Mark said. "I'll pick up a tape recorder before I hit the road, and I'll record my thoughts on my drive to Columbus."

"One other thing I'd like to run by you guys," Josh added. "With two kids and living on a teacher's salary and a nurse's pay, my wife and I struggle to make ends meet. I've been looking for ways to make some extra money and have even toyed around with the idea of writing a book. But so far, I haven't come up with a topic. Now it's like a light bulb went off, and I'm thinking that there's some great material here for my book. If you two have no objections, I'd like to take a stab at it. My working title will be *The Pep Talk*."

"Object?" Johnny shouted. "That's a wonderful idea."

"I'm all for it too, Josh," Mark said. "When you write up The Pep Talk with our combined input, I am certain you'll have a dynamite message. As a matter of fact, I'd like to share it with the bank's management team. You're an articulate man, so I'll tell you what, Josh. You write it up, and I'll have you be the bank's guest speaker at a two-day retreat we're having for our top executives just before New Year's in Palm Beach. Do you think you could be ready by then?"

"Could I? You bet I will. Put me down as your speaker."

"Not so fast, Josh," Johnny interrupted. "You need an agent. How much will the bank pay Josh, Mitch?"

"I know we paid last year's speaker eight thousand dollars. That sound okay with you, Josh?"

Josh quickly extended his right hand. "Shake on that. It's a done deal."

"I wish you wouldn't have acted so hastily, Josh," Johnny said with a smile. "If you would have let me negotiate for you, I could have gotten you ten thousand dollars."

"You do a good job at the retreat," Mark said, "and we'll book you at four more of our division retreats next year, at eight thousand dollars a pop. We're always looking for motivational speakers, and with this material you'll be a superstar."

"I appreciate your vote of confidence in me, Mitch, and I won't let you down."

"Hey, what about Alpha Technology? I want you in Orlando in early January to speak at our annual sales meeting," Johnny said. "We've already booked a speaker, but I can add you to the agenda. Giving The Pep Talk will kick off our new year."

"My turn to be Josh's agent," Mark said. "Josh's speaking services will cost you nine thousand dollars, Johnny."

"That okay with you, Josh?" Johnny asked.

"Let's shake on it."

"Okay, it's a deal," Johnny said. "Nine Gs it is. Too bad Mitch didn't let me finish. I was going to pay you twelve thousand dollars."

The three men laughed and when the check came, Josh said, "Please, the coffee's on me." He grinned and added, "After all, I'm fixing to come into some money.

"But wait, one more thing. When you send me your recollections of The Pep Talk, I'd like you to include how you applied its lessons throughout your careers. For instance, Mr. Christopher talked a lot about teamwork. Do you remember how he talked about trusting everyone to do his assignment?"

"Excellent idea," Johnny nodded. "I also recall that Mr. Christopher talked about love. Now you don't hear that word mentioned at the business seminars or at the business schools. I've attended management courses at the Harvard Business School, for instance, and nobody there is talking to anyone about how you should love your employees. Having said that, I practice it every day in my work. I don't walk the floor giving bear hugs to my workers and telling them how much I love them, of course. If I did, they'd think I was nuts. But love can be expressed in other ways. I do it by paying them good salaries, providing them with excellent fringe benefits and a good working environment, and by giving them wonderful opportunities for advancement."

"Amen," Mark said. "Love is also expressed in the way a manager shows respect to his people. For example, I listen to people. I know this may sound like a simple thing, but most managers don't take the time to hear what their people have to say. All too often executives think they know all the answers and that the people beneath them aren't smart enough to tell them anything

COFFEE AT THE DINER

they don't already know. But the truth is, nobody knows their jobs better than the people on the floor who do it eight hours a day, every workday of the year. So if a manager wants answers, there's where he should go. His own people have the answers. There's no need to bring in outside consultants; just listen to your own people. Now in my humble opinion," Mark continued, "listening is a form of showing people respect. They feel you respect them because you take the time to hear what they have to say. This is not rocket science. It's good management.

LISTENING IS A FORM
OF SHOWING PEOPLE RESPECT

"A manager has to care about his people, and when he does, they respond by caring back. And they do their best work because they don't want to let him down. Like Jesus told us in Mark 10:45, 'The Son of Man came not to be served but to serve.' I take this passage very seriously because I feel my biggest job as CEO is to serve others. Sure, I know most bosses think that because they're the top dog, they are entitled to be served by their subordinates. To my way of thinking, they've got things confused. It's the other way around. I believe my number one priority is to serve the employees in my company. Now when I serve our managers and they in turn serve others within the company, this attitude permeates our organization and extends beyond our building to our customers and suppliers. The end result is high employee loyalty and a lower turnover of people, plus higher customer loyalty that in turn generates repeat orders."

Josh started applauding. "Right on, right on."

"Well, so much for my lesson in Management 101," Mark blushed.

"I agree with everything you say, Mitch," Johnny said. "Jesus devoted His life to serving others. This was epitomized at the Last Supper when He knelt to wash the feet of His disciples. I haven't washed anyone's feet lately, but like you, Mitch, I, too, believe my job as CEO is to serve my people."

"I can see why you two have been so successful," Josh said. "Please be sure to include how you apply the lessons from The Pep Talk in your business careers when you send your recollections to me. I believe that the message from Mr. Christopher's pep talk was intended to stay with us long after we stopped playing football. Now we are responsible for passing it along to others."

"Say, Josh, while you're at it," Mark said, "when you write up The Pep Talk for your lecture, I'd like it if you could make a list that summarizes its important lessons. I'll use the list as a teaser when I talk to my marketing people about your presentation."

"Consider it done," Josh said. "I'll send a copy to you too, Johnny."

"Great. Now if you don't mind, fellas, let's wrap this up," Johnny said. "Mitch will have a professional investigation conducted on Mr. Christopher to see what we can dig up on him. And if he's still alive and well, we'll see if we can talk to him. Agreed? Good. Second, Mitch has his math guys run the numbers so we know the probabilities of something like this happening. Third, my technology guys at Alpha will do an extensive search, both on any other life-changing pep talks in the past, and for other sports articles that might make references relating to Scripture. Maybe if we do enough digging, we'll discover that this isn't as uncommon as it appears to be. Finally, Josh will reconstruct The Pep Talk based on all of our recollections of it."

"Let's not let too much grass grow under our feet before we meet again," Mark said. "Check your calendars the first thing on Monday morning, and if you both can work it in, let's shoot for the weekend before Thanksgiving when we get together. I suggest that we meet in Columbus, which of course is convenient for Josh and me. Does that work for you, Johnny?"

"I'll make it work," Johnny answered.

On the way home from their meeting, Josh's drive seemed considerably shorter. It was the same distance, but this time the high school history teacher was riding on a definite high. In fact, if he could harness the adrenalin shooting through his veins right now, Josh knew he would have enough energy to fuel a 747. He could hardly contain his excitement. He was elated with the reunion with his old friends, and enthralled with the mystery of Mr. Christopher.

What a day. Less than six hours ago his biggest worry was paying for his daughter's orthodontia. Now, Josh's money problems would soon be behind him. It was an awesome, incredible relief. He could hardly wait to break the news to Sarah, but there was too much rural Ohio around him for his cell phone to pick up reception. Josh would simply have to wait until he was in range. Finally, in the vicinity of Columbus, Josh speed-dialed her so he could relay what all had transpired on this most remarkable day.

"Hi, honey," Sarah said. "You must be exhausted. I want to hear all about your day, but before you tell me about it, I have some exciting news that I'm dying to tell you. For starters, I've got a job working evenings at The Limited between Thanksgiving and Christmas. Second, I talked to Dr. Sharp and I asked him if we could pay for Maggie's braces in installments. We talked for a while, and he agreed we could pay $222.22 a month for the next thirty-six months, and with no interest. I can't believe it. Isn't he the nicest man? Now can your good news top that?"

"Well, for starters," Josh answered, "you can tell Dr. Sharp that we deeply appreciate his generosity. But if he'll be kind enough to wait until mid-January, we'll just pay him off in full."

"I'm not following you, Josh," she replied. "Unless you won the lottery today, exactly how do you propose we come up with eight thousand dollars by mid-January?"

"Because by then, my loving wife, our money problems will be behind us."

"It sounds wonderful, darling," Sarah replied, "and as you can imagine, I am quite interested in knowing what has happened to make that possible. Did you come across a long, lost relative in Lincoln who is very rich and of whom I have no knowledge?"

"It's a long story, Sarah, but here goes . . ." Josh began.

PIECING TOGETHER
THE PUZZLE

Josh Goldman spent most of the day on Saturday putting together what he remembered about The Pep Talk. He was surprised at how much he retained over the past three decades. All together he had twelve pages of single-spaced notes, which included two pages about how he applied lessons from The Pep Talk to his teaching position. He wondered if Johnny and Mitch could have possibly matched what he was able to summon up. Sarah read his notes and was astonished that he could recall so much detail. She was equally impressed with the content.

"This is wonderful material," she commented. "It has a message for everyone. Truthfully, I was anticipating some sort of typical pep talk that I imagined coaches gave to their players before a game. This is nothing like I expected. The hospital administrators could surely apply this message. And the doctors I work with, boy do they need it."

"Can you see how any of Mr. Christopher's pep talk has rubbed off on me?" he asked sheepishly.

"I absolutely can," she said, adding, "Mr. Ohio Teacher of the Year."

"Seriously, honey. Tell me something concrete."

"Well, for starters, you live by Mr. Christopher's words when he told the team to 'seize the day.' Indeed you live by the philosophy that dictates: 'This is my day, and I will make the most out of it.'"

"Do you really think that's what I do?" Josh asked sheepishly.

"Absolutely," Sarah continued. "This philosophy is deeply engrained in your brain. You even walk around singing the lyrics to Tim McGraw's song, 'Live Like You Were Dying'— the one about the man in his early forties who just received X-rays from the doctor and has been told he's dying.

"Yeah, I love that he never gave up!" said Josh, with renewed excitement. "In fact, he climbed mountains, jumped out of planes, and went fishing when he could have just as easily given up. But instead, he decided to enjoy all the things he had taken for granted, like his family and his friends, and to live each day as it came—never knowing if it might be his last."

"And how many times have I heard you comment on the expression 'Today is the first day of the rest of your life,' saying that you'd prefer people to ask the question, 'What if today was the *last* day of your life?'"

"Yeah, I do say that quite a bit. What else?"

"I've heard you tell that story about the holy man and the scorpion at least a thousand times," she said, "and how many times do you use the expression afterward, 'This is what I do'?"

"I suppose I have said that on occasion, and yes, I suppose I picked it up at The Pep Talk. Anything else?"

"I truly believe that you're such a wonderful teacher because you expect so much of your students," she answered. "You set a high standard for them, and consequently, they tend to over-achieve so they won't disappoint you."

Sarah paused and hugged her husband. "Promise me that you'll never give up teaching, because it truly is your calling."

"I promise you, honey. I'll always be a teacher," Josh assured her. "Because—to quote myself—'this is what I do.'"

When Josh checked his e-mail on Monday evening, his messages from Johnny and Mark were waiting to be opened. Both men attached long, detailed documents. His two friends had done well; Johnny forwarded thirteen single-spaced typed pages; Mitch had a fifteen-page document, also neatly presented. Judging from their professional-looking formats he received—typo-free—Josh concluded that his two friends had obviously delegated the typing to an assistant. Of course, he had written and typed his document himself. After printing the documents, Josh laid them beside his and began comparing notes. He was astounded to observe how similar the documents were. Although he had no way of knowing it, their combined efforts had covered everything that Mr. Christopher had said to the team.

Studying the three documents, he was overjoyed to discover that The Pep Talk had even more meat to it than he had anticipated. Josh believed its message was not intended to be given only to high school football players—it contained valuable lessons to be able to succeed in any endeavor. He was also convinced that its message could be delivered to a mature audience. Josh would reconstruct it from all of their notes, and when it was completed, he would be prepared to serve as its messenger to the world. Josh suddenly felt as if he had a mission in life, much like he did when he received his first teaching assignment. He could feel the fire in his belly. It was wonderful.

SURROUND YOURSELF WITH ENTHUSIASTIC PEOPLE.

On the subject of fire in the belly, Johnny devoted nearly a full page to how The Pep Talk had fired him up and, consequently, how it had inspired him to play at a peak performance throughout the entire game. He emphasized how he and his teammates had played the game of their lives. "When I interview potential candidates for key managerial positions," his notes revealed, "I look for individuals who possess this quality. I believe it is so essential in the workplace that I've been known to hire a candidate with fire in the belly but with a less impressive résumé instead of a more qualified person who lacks this quality. Frankly, I have an aversion to lukewarm people. I like to be surrounded with people who are enthusiastic and have passion."

When Josh read Johnny's comment about fire in the belly, he remembered how the players held hands in the huddles. He recalled how Johnny kept inspiring everyone to be totally focused on his assignment. "Be so focused you can read the letters on the ball as it spirals into your hands," he told his receivers. "Master your box," he encouraged each offensive lineman. "Everyone do your assignment," he repeated throughout the game.

Reading Johnny's notes, Josh recalled John 20:29: "Blessed are those who have not seen and yet have come to believe." Remembering Mr. Christopher repeating this scripture to the team, Josh realized that Johnny's leadership during the game epitomized the meaning of this verse. As the team's quarterback, Johnny inspired the offensive unit to function as a team, trusting each player to execute his assignment, and together they prevailed over an otherwise superior opponent. Johnny's belief in his linemen—trusting them to defend him against the bigger, stronger Jacktown players—inspired them to believe they could outplay their opponent. He believed they could do what they had never been able to do before. His faith gave them faith in themselves. They didn't want to disappoint him because he believed in them.

Likewise, in the business arena, this same brand of leadership enabled Johnny to found and build Alpha Technology, a company that ultimately grew into a major high-tech company. Here too, Johnny believed in the unseen. Josh thought about how Johnny had built Alpha from scratch, and he envisioned how his friend faced and overcame seemingly insurmountable obstacles along the way. How difficult it must have been in the beginning stages to convince capable people to give up more secure jobs where they were employed to join his small startup company. In light of how many startups never get off the ground, he considered it remarkable that they would do so with no assurances that Alpha would someday survive, let alone thrive.

Equally difficult was the task of raising money from investors, persuading them to invest in a company without a track record. Obviously to win over employees and investors, they had to believe in Alpha's future—and most importantly in Johnny Corleone. They had to believe in the picture of the future that Johnny painted. *This is what strong leadership is*, Josh surmised. Three cheers for his friend Johnny Corleone, founder and CEO of Alpha Technology!

Mark wrote a single-spaced page dissertation on accountability in business, an important lesson that he took from The Pep Talk and applied throughout his entire career. "Like a football team," he wrote, "in every organization each member contributes to the whole, and every successful outcome must be attributed to all of the members." He went on to explain how every department has its own area of responsibility, and the success of the entire organization depends on the combined performances of all departments. If one member isn't doing his or her assignment, it affects the entire department. "If, for instance, the sales reps are producing large orders, what good is it if the plant falls behind on production and is unable to fulfill orders? The same is true if the accounting department fails to send invoices or collect payments due the company. Every individual and every department must be held accountable. In business, everyone must pull together; a total team effort is required."

Josh observed how all three of them elaborated on the importance of believing in a positive outcome. "Never view your competition as a giant, and in comparison, see yourself as a grasshopper," Johnny wrote. Mark quoted Joshua 1:9: "Be strong and courageous; do not be frightened or dismayed; for the LORD your God is with you wherever you go." Here, Mark emphasized how he believed that with God on his side, he was bound to succeed in all endeavors. *What a wonderful attitude*, Josh thought. "No wonder Mitch does so well," he told Sarah.

Mark recalled the story about the college student who was able to solve the two problems his professor wrote on the class blackboard that even stumped Albert Einstein. Mark stressed, "The point is, you can achieve anything you believe you can achieve. When I started at the bank, I believed I could attain every promotion that I eventually received. Now, when I started at a low entry level, I wasn't thinking how I would someday be the bank's CEO. Instead I set my sights on becoming an assistant branch manager, and once I received that promotion, I focused doing what was necessary to become the branch manager. I did this throughout my career when I became a district manager, a regional manager, assistant vice president, vice president, and so on as I worked my way up the corporate ladder. While it's a positive thing to think big, I focused on one step at a time. That's what Mr. Christopher instructed us to do—focus on each play, one at a time. Had we only been focused on the scoreboard, we wouldn't have exercised our given assignments on each individual play. The same is applicable in business."

Mark elaborated that under his guidance State National had a master plan to expand by acquiring banks in small towns throughout Ohio. In addition, it planned to acquire small and medium-sized regional banks. "Here, too, it was one acquisition at a time. Or as Mr. Christopher said, 'One play at a time, and the scoreboard will take care of itself.' I always thought beyond the present into the future, and I was never preoccupied with short-term profits. In business, there are times when it is necessary to incur short-term losses so that long-term gains can be realized."

> RUN ONE PLAY AT A TIME, AND THE FINAL SCORE
> WILL TAKE CARE OF ITSELF.

Josh correctly assessed Mr. Christopher's pep talk as a lesson on facing adversity. It had a deeper meaning than preparing a football team to face an awesome foe the likes of the Jacktown Giants. He had told the players to expect adversity in the game, that they would face it together, and most importantly, they would be there for each other. He stressed that knowing they were not alone and could trust each other would serve as a source of strength; together they could overcome their adversary.

SUCCESS IS GOING FROM FAILURE TO FAILURE WITHOUT FAILING.

The team's ultimate win over Jacktown would stay with them for a lifetime. It was tangible proof that it is possible to confront insurmountable odds and be victorious. Having experienced a feat of this magnitude at an early age was indeed a blessing. *There is nothing like learning an invaluable lesson by actually doing it,* Josh thought to himself.

The twenty-four-game losing streak that his team suffered prior to its victory over Jacktown also flashed in his mind. He marveled at the fact that the team could be knocked down—no, not just knocked down, but crushed—game after game and still suit up and face next Friday night's opponent. *That is what makes football such a terrific sport,* he mused. *Every play results in young boys getting knocked down, and afterward, they must lift themselves off the ground even though they may be knocked down again.* This by itself is a wonderful lesson in life because life itself is a series of many defeats. Resiliency is a wonderful trait to acquire as a young person. The secret of success, Josh wrote down in his notes, is to possess the ability to endure defeat after defeat without allowing yourself to be defeated. Another way to say it, he deliberated, would be: Success is going from failure to failure without failing.

By the middle of the week, Josh had reconstructed the entire pep talk and forwarded it to Johnny and Mark. His e-mail also included a list of twelve important lessons contained in The Pep Talk:

1. Don't defeat yourself before you get started by allowing negative thoughts about past events burden you with limitations. As Carl Sandburg wrote, "The past is a bucket of ashes." Rid yourself of self-doubt. Don't allow yourself to be defeated by preconceptions.

2. Seize the moment. In a pivotal moment you can choose to say, "This is my day, and I will make the most of it."

3. Nobody succeeds without the help of others. It takes a team effort. Trust others to do their jobs. The combined effort of everyone executing his or her job produces superior results.

4. Stay focused. Don't focus on the scoreboard; the final score will take care of itself. In business, don't be preoccupied with how much money you will make. Concentrate on your task at hand—the money will come.

5. Visualize your success. This will give you a goal that you will eventually attain.

6. Adversity is part of life. Don't let setbacks defeat you. Adversity makes you stronger.

7. Be persistent. Never, never give in.

8. Expect the competition to be strong. Don't underestimate an opponent.

9. Believe in others and others will believe in you.

10. Be a team player.

11. Believe and trust the process. Rid yourself of self-doubts.

12. Believe you will succeed. Have faith in your future (the unseen).

On Thursday evening Josh received a phone call from Johnny Corleone. "Congratulations on doing an amazing job," Johnny said to him. "I felt like I was listening to Mr. Christopher when I read it. And your list of the twelve important lessons was right on target. By the way, I had a long talk with Stan Howard, our VP of Marketing and told him everything—Mr. Christopher's pep talk, the game, last week's reunion with Coach Morris in Lincoln, and what the three of us are doing in regards to the re-creation of The Pep Talk. He's as excited about all of this as we are. He put you in the program to address our sales team in Orlando on January 19, Saturday morning at 10:30. He wants you to speak for forty-five minutes. Does that work for you?"

"Perfect," Josh replied.

"Oh yes, I took the liberty to have Katie Wilson, my executive assistant, book a reservation for you departing Columbus early Friday evening. I assume you are planning on bringing Sarah, so Katie booked her too. You are bringing her, aren't you, Josh?"

"I will, and I know how thrilled she'll be," Josh replied.

"Katie reserved a room for you at Four Seasons. I'm looking forward to meeting Sarah."

"Hey, before you hang up," Josh inquired, "what did your math whizzes come up with regarding the probabilities?"

"They're still working on it," Johnny said, "so we'll have to wait and see. They're also doing searches on the Internet to see if they can find articles that have biblical references. They've come across thousands of them, so they're checking them out, one by one. It will take some time to see if any are meaningful. I'll keep you posted. Ciao."

As soon as Josh put down the receiver, he rushed into the kitchen to tell Sarah, "Johnny Corleone confirmed that I will be speaking in Orlando on January 19."

"Thank you, dear God," Sarah said, embracing her husband, her eyes looking skyward.

"The fees from the speech alone cover Maggie's braces," Josh replied, giving her a big squeeze. "Oh, one other thing. You're going too."

Two hours later Mark called. "Sorry to get back to you at this late hour, Josh, but when Janie saw how excited I was when I came home tonight, she wanted to know why, so I told her about The Pep Talk. Then she insisted that I read it to her after dinner. Janie and I are both ecstatic about what you did with our notes. It's quite impressive work. We've got something very special here, my friend."

"I'm thrilled you like it so much," Josh said.

"By the way, our people have started their investigation on Mr. Christopher. No leads as of today, but remember, patience is a virtue. If he's out there, they'll find him.

"One other thing," Mark added. "Before I left the office I talked to my vice president who's in charge of the retreat we're having at the end of the year. I told him I wanted you to address our management team. Mark December 28 and 29 on your calendar, Josh. That's the Tuesday and Wednesday between Christmas and New Year's. You said you could make it. I'm hoping that works for you."

"Definitely," Josh said excitedly.

"It's at The Breakers in Palm Beach. Someone from the bank will call you in a day or so with the details."

"Excellent," Josh said.

Everything was beginning to fall into place for Josh Goldman. His money problems would soon be behind him. He was making great headway with the writing of *The Pep Talk*. And, perhaps best of all, Josh had a new lease on life because he felt that what he was doing would have a positive influence on the lives of many people. "Life is good for this Ohio schoolteacher," he told his wife, Sarah.

On Friday afternoon, November 26, Josh received an e-mail from Johnny Corleone:

Josh,

Mitch and I compared notes on what we found out about Mr. Christopher and his pep talk. We want to do a phone conference with you and Coach Morris on Wednesday evening, December 1. Does 7:30 next Wednesday work for you? If so, I'll set up a conference call. Let me know. Looking forward to talking to you.

Johnny

On December 1, 2003, the teleconference began promptly at 7:30 p.m.

"Before we get started," Johnny said, "I hope you all had a wonderful Thanksgiving. How was yours, Coach?"

"My daughters and their families visited," Morris replied in a frail voice. "We are blessed with beautiful children and grandchildren."

"I'm here too," Margaret Morris chimed in. "I hope you boys don't mind. Jack wanted me to listen in so in case he missed something, I'd remember it for him."

"Good idea, Mrs. M, and it's always a pleasure to hear your voice. I'm happy to hear you all enjoyed your Thanksgiving," Johnny said warmly. Then, changing hats and sounding very much like a CEO, he explained to Margaret and Jack Morris about how the three of them had stopped at the diner and what they discussed. He also brought them up to date on the investigations that were being conducted by both Alpha and State National. "As you can see, we were as intrigued with what you told us as you were, Coach, and we wanted to see if there was some logical explanation to all of it. The purpose of this conference call is to update you on what we learned."

Johnny stopped in the middle of his thought and said, "Mitch, I don't mean to dominate this conversation. So why don't you give your report first, and afterward I'll follow up with mine."

"I'll be delighted," Mark pitched in. "As you all know, our bank must know about the people we loan money to. I assigned Peter Jefferson, one of our best people at State National, to find out everything there was to know about Mr. Christopher. I gave

Jefferson the information we knew about Mr. Christopher, which admittedly wasn't a whole lot, but when I first gave this information to him he said, 'This is more than enough, Mark. Just give me a day or two, and I'll have plenty to report to you about the man.'"

"Excuse me, for a minute, Mitch," Johnny said, "but didn't Jefferson tell you that in this day and age, making reference to the Internet, that it would be a walk in the park?'"

"In those exact words," Mark concurred. "Now like I said, Peter Jefferson has a reputation for being an outstanding investigator. Five days later Jefferson told me, 'I'm not finding anything on this guy, Mr. Mitchell, but don't you worry, something's got to show up. I have a call into a contact in Philly who promised to get back to me on Monday. If a Mr. Christopher ever existed, we'll soon know all about him.' Well, Jefferson and his associate in Philadelphia didn't come up with jack squat. Finally last week, Jefferson threw in the towel. He told me, 'Mr. Mitchell, it's as if the man never existed. I've never seen anything like it in my entire career, nor for that matter, have any of my colleagues.' So that's my final report. Nada!"

"Thank you so much," Morris said, his voice sounding a bit stronger. "Like I told you boys, while I'm not an expert like the bank's man, I ran into the same thing when I tried to contact Mr. Christopher. It was as if he never existed."

"What happened when Jefferson checked with the Philadelphia Eagles and Cleveland Browns?" Josh asked.

"Did anyone recollect a Mr. Christopher or a stranger giving a pep talk?"

"Nobody recalled anything," Mark answered. "But personnel on both teams said there have been many, many guest speakers over the years, and with the turnover of players and coaches, nobody is around from when Mr. Christopher might have given a pep talk to either team. What's more, neither organization kept any records of guest speakers from so far back."

"Now, for my findings," Johnny said. "I do have some concrete results to report to you. As the three of us agreed at the diner, I volunteered to assign some of my mathematicians at Alpha to determine the probabilities of a man quoting scriptures before a football game was played that were relevant to the names, players' numbers, and playing statistics in the actual game. I'm referring to those articles that you showed us, Coach, when you highlighted Mark 11:24, John 20:29, and Joshua 1:9. Is everyone with me?"

He paused and waited for their assent. "Good. I could give you lists of facts and figures, but to make a long story short, the odds were so astronomically high, there were no odds," Johnny continued. "We're talking about billions to one. I wanted to double-check this, so I contacted Bill Brown, a friend of mine who's a noted actuary at Travelers. Well, he too came up with nada. That's right, zip. Zilch. And he offered no explanation. Not being a man of faith, Brown refused to believe what had happened. He simply concluded that it was impossible. To quote him verbatim: 'It is not possible for a person to prophesy what you claim your Mr. Christopher did.' He insisted that the biblical quotes couldn't have been made before the game and said that The Pep Talk had to have been made *afterwards*. It just wasn't possible, and what undoubtedly happened was that we got the dates wrong.

"'Something is clearly missing that you're not telling me.' he maintained. 'I'm not suggesting that it was intentional. But some of the facts have been omitted.'

"Oh yes, he then went on to say something we had wondered about earlier: 'The Pep Talk quoted John 15:12, but there was no reference to it in any of the newspaper articles. Certainly, this must arouse your suspicions? If this was, as you suggest, God-inspired, why wasn't there a player named John with corresponding numbers 15 and 12 that were also pertinent? Got you there, don't I?' he said."

"I've been thinking about that myself," Josh said.

"And what did you conclude?" Johnny asked.

"My take on it is," Josh answered, "that if we believe in God, we shouldn't expect Him to have to prove Himself. So what happened here is that a piece of the puzzle is intentionally missing. If God wanted us to have absolute, undeniable proof of His existence, we would have had it thousands of years ago."

"Amen," Morris said.

"I'd like to continue with my report," Johnny said. "Being that Alpha is in the high-tech industry and we have access to the top Internet companies, I had some of my people check with our sources to see what might show up regarding another football game or another sporting event that might resemble our experience. Sure, they came up with biblical names like John, Peter, Samuel, Jeremiah, Daniel, and so on. They checked them all out. They even found some chapters and verses that matched numbers pertaining to game statistics. Considering the large numbers of games played over the years, going in we figured that was bound to happen. And on some occasions there were games with scriptures matching players' names with their jersey number as well as their game statistics. Those leads were also followed up but produced no tangible results. There was never more than one in a single game. So they chalked that up to the law of probabilities—never with a Mr. Christopher.

"Now you have to remember, their search only went from the present back to the mid-1950s, a relatively short period of time," Johnny continued. "It would be presumptuous to assume that a similar incident or incidents could not have occurred centuries ago and certainly at a different venue. Instead of on a football field, it could have been on a battlefield, in a debate at the League of Nations, or even on the Roman Senate floor. Perhaps there have been many 'Mr. Christophers,' who came in different attire. Rather than wearing a business suit and a fedora, they wore cloaks, or for that matter, dresses or gowns. Perhaps it was a 'Ms. Christopher' who delivered the message."

"I agree," Josh interjected. "It would be presumptuous for

us to think that what happened at The Pep Talk would be the only format where a phenomenon of this nature could occur. Certainly, we have to give credit to the Good Lord for being creative."

Josh laughed at what he just said. "That's funny. After all, God is our Supreme Creator. Why wouldn't He be creative?"

"Well, guys, this is why it took so long, because initially they limited their search to football games," Johnny added, "and nothing came up that had to do with a pep talk or anything else that could possibly prophesy such exact statistics before a game. Nor did anything show up that had anything to do with Mr. Christopher. Then they started to explore other avenues and again, they drew a blank. As far as our people were concerned, they concluded that this was a one-of-a-kind occurrence—that is, regarding a pep talk and a football game or a sporting event. But when you look at the big picture—over the centuries, there is no way of investigating events that were never recorded."

"Thank you so much," Morris said. "This means so much to me."

"We love you, Coach, but we did it for us too," Mitch said.

"We also have a surprise for you, Coach," Johnny said. "The three of us independently wrote down everything we remember about Mr. Christopher's Pep Talk, and Josh, being the historian on our team, re-created it from all of our recollections."

"You did?" Morris said. "Can I have a copy?"

"As soon as I've completed it, Coach," Josh answered.

Right now, it's a work in progress and in its second draft. I'll finish my third and final draft by Friday."

"In two days? That's wonderful," Morris said.

"I'll overnight it to you for a Saturday delivery," Josh replied.

"Well, where do we go from here; what does this all mean?" Margaret Morris asked. "And what about Mr. Christopher? We know nothing about him. And what about those billions-to-one odds?"

"I choose to believe it was God-inspired," Mark said.

"Mitch is right," Jack Morris said. "I don't understand how this all happened, but I have faith that there is a reason why it happened. And that's good enough for me. For a man in my condition, I can't tell you how comforting that is. All of this reconfirms my belief that I have something wonderful to look forward to when I am no longer of this earth."

"God bless you boys," Margaret Morris said.

On Saturday morning, December 4, 2003, Jack Morris received the first copy of *The Pep Talk*. Although nobody would ever know, it was identical, word for word, to what Mr. Christopher had said.

Jack Morris was sitting in his leather chair behind his desk in his library. He had fallen asleep with his right hand clutching the last page from *The Pep Talk*. Margaret peeked in the room and was happy to see the content expression on his face.

The Pep Talk Revisited

On December 28, 2003, Mark Mitchell, CEO of State National Bank, stood at the podium in a conference room at The Breakers Hotel in Palm Beach, Florida. He was addressing thirty-six senior managers at a morning meeting. It was an enthusiastic group, and Mark was good at firing them up.

"Good morning," he greeted them. "I am delighted to be with you today in sunny Florida." Mark talked for a few minutes about bank business. He then announced, "I am privileged to have the honor of introducing our guest speaker, Josh Goldman, who I promise will tell you something that will be nothing like anything you've ever heard before. My friend Josh and I go way back. We grew up in Lincoln, Ohio, a small former steel mill town near the Pennsylvania and West Virginia borders. Lincoln High was once also known for its powerhouse football teams. But that was way back in the '50s when most of us in this room were not even born.

"In the '70s when Josh and I were Lincoln Lions team-mates," Mark continued, "our team was no powerhouse. At one time, we were riding a twenty-four-game losing streak and were facing the Jacktown Giants—and in our minds they really were giants. They had a forty-two-game winning streak and were the state champions for three consecutive years. But something unusual happened the night before, and we did win that game in undoubtedly the biggest upset in Ohio high school football history."

Mark went on to tell his audience about the stranger who had talked to the team the night before the game. He gave a rundown of the game itself. He was not bashful about telling them about his eleven broken passes and twenty-four tackles. He also talked about Johnny completing twenty out of twenty-nine passes, and pointing a finger at the guest speaker, he described how Josh kicked three field goals, including the winning one with three seconds remaining on the clock. Mark also had the newspaper clippings of the game projected on a screen. Then he showed them copies that had been highlighted and explained how these numbers corresponded with the scripture quoted in The Pep Talk. Next he explained how experts calculated the probabilities in the billions and how they were unable to find the stranger in spite of having what should have been ample information to locate him. Finally, he described the impact that The Pep Talk had on his life as well as on Johnny's and Josh's.

"I'll just say one more thing before our guest speaker takes the floor," Mark said. "If it were not for Mr. Christopher's pep talk, I am certain that my life would have been much different." He paused briefly and added, "I truly believe that I wouldn't be standing here today as the CEO of this company if not for The Pep Talk."

By the time Mark had finished, his audience was on the edge of their seats. "Ladies and gentlemen, I present to you my good friend Josh Goldman who will deliver The Pep Talk as it has been re-created by Josh, Johnny, and yours truly. And while we at State National may not be a football team, I assure you that its message will be as inspiring and meaningful to you as it has been to us."

Josh walked to the podium and stood facing the audience, waiting for the applause to die down. When the room was silent, he said: "There were two buffaloes standing in the open range in Wyoming . . ."

12 BUSINESS LESSONS FROM THE PEP TALK

1. Don't defeat yourself before you get started by allowing negative thoughts about past events burden you with limitations. As Carl Sandburg wrote, "The past is a bucket of ashes." Rid yourself of self-doubt. Don't allow yourself to be defeated by preconceptions.

2. Seize the moment. In a pivotal moment you can choose to say, "This is my day, and I will make the most of it."

3. Nobody succeeds without the help of others. It takes a team effort. Trust others to do their jobs. The combined effort of everyone executing his or her job produces superior results.

4. Stay focused. Don't focus on the scoreboard; the final score will take care of itself. In business, don't be preoccupied with how much money you will make. Concentrate on your task at hand—the money will come.

5. Visualize your success. This will give you a goal that you will eventually attain.

6. Adversity is part of life. Don't let setbacks defeat you. Adversity makes you stronger.

7. Be persistent. Never, never give in.

8. Expect the competition to be strong. Don't underestimate an opponent.

9. Believe in others and others will believe in you.

10. Be a team player.

11. Believe and trust the process. Rid yourself of self-doubts.

12. Believe you will succeed. Have faith in your future (the unseen).

ABOUT THE AUTHORS

KEVIN ELKO went to West Virginia University where he completed a Masters in Counseling, a Masters in Sports Psychology, a Graduate Certificate in Gerontology, and a Doctorate in Education with a major emphasis in Sport and Counseling. He is also a Certified Addictions Counselor. Dr. Elko has been an Adjunct Professor at the University of Pittsburgh School of Medicine and a writer for drkoop.com. He is the author of *Nerves of Steel*.

Dr. Elko has consulted with and presented to many companies and organizations including: Travelers Insurance Company, Merrill Lynch, Smith Barney, Prudential Securities, Abbott Diagnostics, Smith Kline Beecham, and The Young Presidents Organization. He has spoken to and counseled many sports organizations including: the Dallas Cowboys, the New Orleans Saints, the Buffalo Bills, the Pittsburgh Steelers, the Cleveland Browns, the Pittsburgh Penguins, the Miami

Dolphins and the Philadelphia Eagles. He has also worked with many high-ranking college football teams including: the Miami Hurricanes, the LSU Tigers, the Pittsburgh Panthers, and the Nebraska Cornhuskers.

Each year Dr. Elko addresses between 150 and 200 audiences. With hundreds of standing ovations, he is one of America's top motivational speakers. He and his wife Karen have two children and live in Presto, Pennsylvania not far from Pittsburgh.

To learn more about Dr. Kevin Elko visit:
www.nervesofsteel.net.

ROBERT L. SHOOK has been a full-time author for 30 years and has authored more than 50 books. Several of his books have appeared on the *New York Times'* best sellers list, including *Longaberger: An American Success Story*, a number-one bestseller. Other books include: *Miracle Medicines*, *Winning the NFL Way*, *Doing Business by the Good Book*, and *The IBM Way*. His most current publication is *The Customer Rules*. Mr. Shook is one of America's premier business writers. *The Pep Talk* is his first work of fiction. A graduate of Ohio State University, Mr. Shook resides in Columbus, Ohio with his wife, Elinor.

To learn more about Robert L. Shook and his other books,
visit www.Shookbook.com.

Elko and Shook plan to collaborate on another book in the not-too-distant future.

ACKNOWLEDGMENTS

We were blessed to have a wonderful team of people who contributed to the making of this book. First, we thank RJ Shook who thought the two of us should write a book about pep talks. We are indebted to RJ for introducing us to each other and his urging us to collaborate. Had it not been for this introduction, this book would not have been written.

We were blessed to have supportive wives who never complained when we spent hundreds of hours talking long-distance, oftentimes late at night and on weekends. Karen and Elinor, you're the best.

We thank Cleveland Brown's former head coach Butch Davis and the University of Miami's former head coach Larry Coker for giving permission to Bob to sit in on pep talks that Kevin gave to their respective teams as well as allowing him to watch games from the playing field.

Early on, when some people in the publishing industry

didn't think we should write a work of fiction, Charlie Morgan, a wonderful man and an excellent attorney who knows how to put deals together was one of our early supporters. Without Charlie's guidance, it's unlikely that this book would have happened. You're a good man, Charlie Morgan.

We extend a special acknowledgment to the McBride Literary Agency, headed by Margret McBride, a very capable woman who was also an early believer in our story. We are grateful to the agency's vice president, Donna DeGutis, who sold our manuscript to Thomas Nelson, Inc., a house that we truly believe is the perfect publisher for this book.

There are several excellent people at Thomas Nelson that did outstanding work. First, there is Victor Oliver, who acquired the book; Victor is a legendry figure in publishing circles—we feel privileged to be associated with a man of his stature. The same is true for our publisher, Joel Miller, a respected professional in publishing circles. We thank Joel for assigning senior editor Kristen Parish to work with us. Kristen's guidance was invaluable and much appreciated. Our associate editor, Heather Skelton, is a sheer delight to work with. She is bright and insightful; her upbeat enthusiasm is contagious. We also thank Amanda Hope Haley who did an excellent copyediting job and Mandi Cofer who designed the book—the first-rate job she did is evidenced for all to see.

There are many good books that never reach their potential sales figures due to inadequate marketing efforts. This will not happen with The Pep Talk because we have three exceptional people on our team: Damon Goude, a highly-skilled marketing director; Curt Harding, a very talented publicist, and Janice Babbs, an energetic, creative marketing specialist. Thank you, Damon, Curt, and Janice for your support. It is very much appreciated.

A special thanks goes to Debbie Watts who transcribed many cassettes containing pep talks; Debbie always does exceptional work; she is a good friend whose support is always appreciated.

Like the fictitious Lincoln Lions in our story, when everyone works together as a team, good things happen.